PL/T:
A TUTORIAL PROGRAMMING SYSTEM
IN TURBO PASCAL

COMPUTER SCIENCE TEXTS

COMPUTER SCIENCE TEXTS

PL/T:
A Tutorial Programming System in TURBO Pascal

N. J. FIDDIAN
MSc, PhD
Department of Computing Mathematics
Mathematics Institute
University College
Cardiff

BLACKWELL SCIENTIFIC PUBLICATIONS
OXFORD LONDON EDINBURGH
BOSTON PALO ALTO MELBOURNE

For in much wisdom is much grief; and he that increaseth knowledge
increaseth sorrow.

Ecclesiastes 1:18

© 1986 by
Blackwell Scientific Publications
Editorial offices:
Osney Mead, Oxford OX2 0EL
8 John Street, London WC1N 2ES
23 Ainslie Place, Edinburgh EH3 6AJ
52 Beacon Street, Boston
  Massachusetts 02108, USA
667 Lytton Avenue, Palo Alto
  California 94301, USA
107 Barry Street, Carlton
  Victoria 3053, Australia

First published 1986

Set by Getset (Bowden Typesetting
Services) Ltd Eynsham, Oxford.
Printed and bound in Great Britain

DISTRIBUTORS

USA and Canada
  Blackwell Scientific Publications Inc
  PO Box 50009, Palo Alto
  California 94303

Australia
  Blackwell Scientific Publications
    (Australia) Pty Ltd
  107 Barry Street,
  Carlton, Victoria 3053

British Library
Cataloguing in Publication Data

Fiddian, N.J.
  PL/T—a tutorial programming system in
  TURBO Pascal.—(Computer science texts)
  1. Turbo Pascal (Computer program language)
  I. Title II. Series
  055. 13′3   QA76.73

ISBN 0-632-01634-5
ISBN 0-632-01635-3 Pbk

Contents

Chapter 1

Introduction to the PL/T Programming System

A *compiler* is a system program whose purpose is to translate user programs written in a high-level programming language such as Pascal, known as the *source* language, into equivalent programs in a relatively low-level object or *target* language. Typically, the target language will be either the binary machine language of some real computer, directly executable by the CPU of that computer, or the machine language of a simpler, hypothetical computer specially designed to make the compiler's translation targetting task easier, which can then be executed by a *machine language interpreter* program running on a real machine. The latter approach is used in a number of contemporary programming systems [1], notably the so-called Pascal P-Code systems [2, 3, 4].

In a few programming systems the compilation task is split between two complementary compiler programs, the first of which specializes solely in the detection of source language errors and is called a *syntax checker*. The second program, the compiler proper, is then free to concentrate on translation *per se* of source programs which are known to be correct. Splitting results in both programs becoming smaller and simpler than a combined compiler.

This handbook presents in detail a syntax checker, compiler and machine language interpreter for a very simple Pascal-like programming language called PL/T—Tiny Programming Language. It includes definitions of the PL/T source language and imaginary target machine and complete listings of the associated compiler and interpreter programs written in Pascal. The principal aim of the book is to capture and communicate, by means of a complete, concrete example suitable for study at introductory course level, the essence of what goes on inside the program compilation/execution 'black box', with particular emphasis on the representations and transformations involved. A secondary aim is to expose the reader through system source code examination to a variety of data, procedure and control constructs at work in a realistic (non-trivial) program setting.

The book is intended primarily for first course students of computer science who have some experience of Pascal programming and an understanding of the basic principles of stored program computer operation. Familiarity with syntax diagrams as a language definition formalism is also

1

assumed. PL/T is loosely based on the PL/0 system of Niklaus Wirth (described in his book *Algorithms + Data Structures = Programs* [5]), but has been extensively modified to suit less advanced audiences in a short course timescale, and to take advantage of the interaction and soft-copy display capabilities of modern computer systems, including floppy-disc-based microcomputer systems. Stringent simplification of the resultant software to make it as easy as possible to understand means that the PL/T source language is necessarily extremely limited but it is still practicable (and challenging!) to write useful test programs in it.

The PL/T system, written in TURBO™ Pascal, is available for purchase from Blackwell Scientific Publications Ltd in the form of three programs: a 'sudden death' syntax checker (for introductory study but not for serious use), a syntax checker incorporating error recovery (essential to use, not intended for study), and an integrated compiler/machine language interpreter program (for use and study) which assumes error-free source input and produces optional mnemonic displays of machine code generation and target program execution as they occur. The flavour of system operation is conveyed by compilation/ execution listing extracts for a sample PL/T test program which may be found in the Appendix. Although not absolutely necessary, the system software as such complements this handbook by allowing direct 'hands-on' use of the programs concerned while they are being studied. In addition to this supporting practical role, it may also be employed as an ideal basis for system extension project work in more advanced courses covering the same subject area.

TURBO™ Pascal is a registered trade mark of Borland International Inc.

Chapter 2

Programming in PL/T Source Language

Because of its particular role, to act as a vehicle for use in demonstrating an ultra-simple tutorial programming system, the PL/T source language is absolutely minimal: the only facilities it provides are those without which it would be impossible to write any useful programs at all. These are variable declaration, arithmetic expression and assignment of integer type only (it is also possible to define named integer constants), together with the three fundamental control constructs of sequence, selection and repetition (the last two involving simple Boolean expressions). The precise form of language used in each case is identical with that of Pascal except in one or two minor respects (e.g. integer type specification in variable declarations is implicit and "/" represents integer division). A detailed description of the language, covering lexical and syntactic aspects separately, is given in Chapters 5 and 6. Figure 2.1 shows a typical PL/T source program (reproduced from the Appendix).

Among the facilities the PL/T source language does *not* offer are data types other than integer, any data structuring facilities, additional control constructs such as REPEAT and CASE, procedures/functions and explicit input/output. Program heading (PROGRAM) statements are also omitted and IF statements are not allowed to have an ELSE part. There are no labels or GOTO statements. The example below is therefore representative of the entire language.

```
{A PL/T PROGRAM TO COUNT DIGITS IN A NUMBER}

CONST RADIX=10;
VAR   NUMBER,DCOUNT;

BEGIN NUMBER:=0; {SIMULATE INPUT OF NUMBER BY ASSIGNMENT}
      DCOUNT:=0; {INITIALISE DIGIT COUNT}
      IF NUMBER=0 THEN DCOUNT:-1; {NUMBER 0 IS A SPECIAL CASE}
      WHILE NUMBER<>0 DO {LOOP TO COUNT DIGITS WHILE ANY LEFT}
      BEGIN NUMBER:=NUMBER/RADIX; DCOUNT:=DCOUNT+1
      END
      {DCOUNT CONTAINS THE DESIRED RESULT}
END.
```

Fig. 2.1. A sample PL/T program.

Lest the reader should be at a loss to think of any, some further example programs which fall within the limited scope of the language include calculation of GCD (greatest common divisor) and NCR (binomial coefficient) values, number reversal (e.g. 123 → 321), and testing whether or not numbers are prime. These and other examples are set as exercises at the end of the book.

Chapter 3

Overview of Syntax Checker and Compiler Programs

The aim of this chapter and the following one is to serve as an architectural commentary on the programs that together comprise the PL/T system. These are two syntax checkers—one crude (PARSER0), and one sophisticated (PARSER)—and a combined compiler/machine interpreter program (COMPILXEC), as described in the PL/T software release summary (Chapter 9). We concentrate primarily here on COMPILXEC, since this embraces PARSER0 as a subset and PARSER is not intended for source code study in the context of this treatise. The clear logical separation between compiler and interpreter parts of COMPILXEC is recognized by considering the former in this chapter and the latter in Chapter 4. Relevant source listings of PARSER0 and COMPILXEC (including INTERPRET) may be found at the end of this handbook; they can also be displayed or printed as software release files. A useful Index to the main sections and routines in both programs is provided with their handbook listings. Although PARSER, the sophisticated syntax checker, is excluded from detailed study consideration because error recovery is a relatively advanced subject, its structure and content as a program is otherwise very similar to PARSER0. A source listing of PARSER is therefore included with the two study listings for interest and completeness.

We begin consideration of COMPILXEC with Figure 3.1, which portrays the architecture of this program in terms of a hierarchy of modules—groups of logically related procedure/function routines—and principal information flow (PARSER0 is essentially the same, excluding the code generation and PL/T program execution sections of the hierarchy). Followed top down, this hierarchy is the key to understanding the source code of COMPILXEC (or PARSER0).

At the heart of the figure (its central sub-tree, below COMPILE), attention is focused on the three fundamental phases of COMPILXEC: lexical analysis, syntax analysis/code synthesis, and code generation; through which, in order, source language input is progressively transformed into target language output. Each of these phases will be examined in more detail below. The function of the other modules of the compiler section of COMPILXEC should be self-explanatory from their source code so these will not be described further, save to note that initialization includes, among other things, the establishment of reserved word and lexical character-into-symbol mapping tables, and that interfacing with the user includes production of a generated target program summary in mnemonic (assembly language-like) form as a final compilation act.

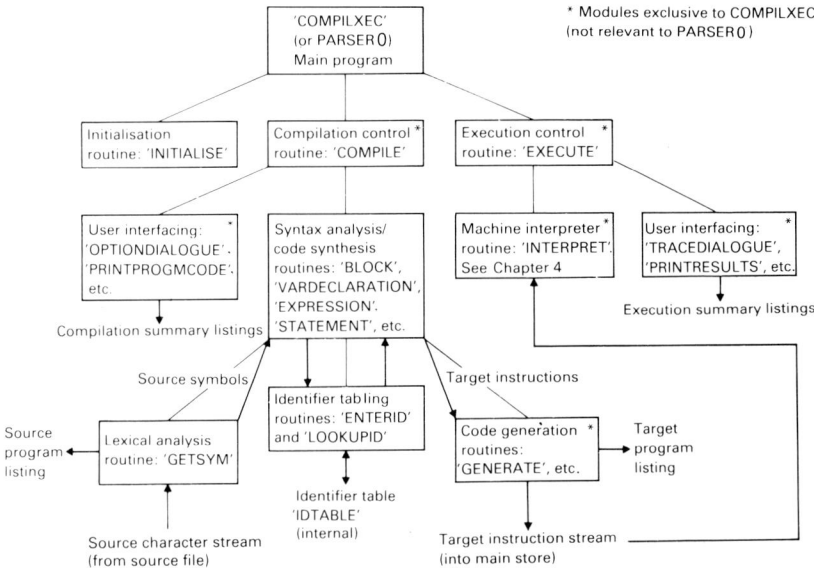

Fig.3.1. COMPILXEC (or PARSER0) module hierarchy (——) and information flow (—→).

Lexical analysis

The main purpose of the lexical analysis phase of a compiler is to recognize symbols, i.e. to identify clusters of characters in the source input character stream which correspond to individual source vocabulary elements such as identifiers, numbers, operators and punctuation marks (as defined in Chapter 5). This is illustrated in Figure 3.2a (lower half) and works on a one symbol at a time basis as the figure shows. In addition, the lexical analyser (GETSYM) looks after such matters as source program listing, skipping of spaces and comments and distinguishing between identifiers and reserved words. A binary search algorithm is used for reserved word table look-up. The result produced each time GETSYM is invoked is the unique classification code

(SYM, of type SYMBOL) of the next source input symbol, augmented in the case of identifier and number symbols by the corresponding name character string (ID) or numerical value (NUM), respectively.

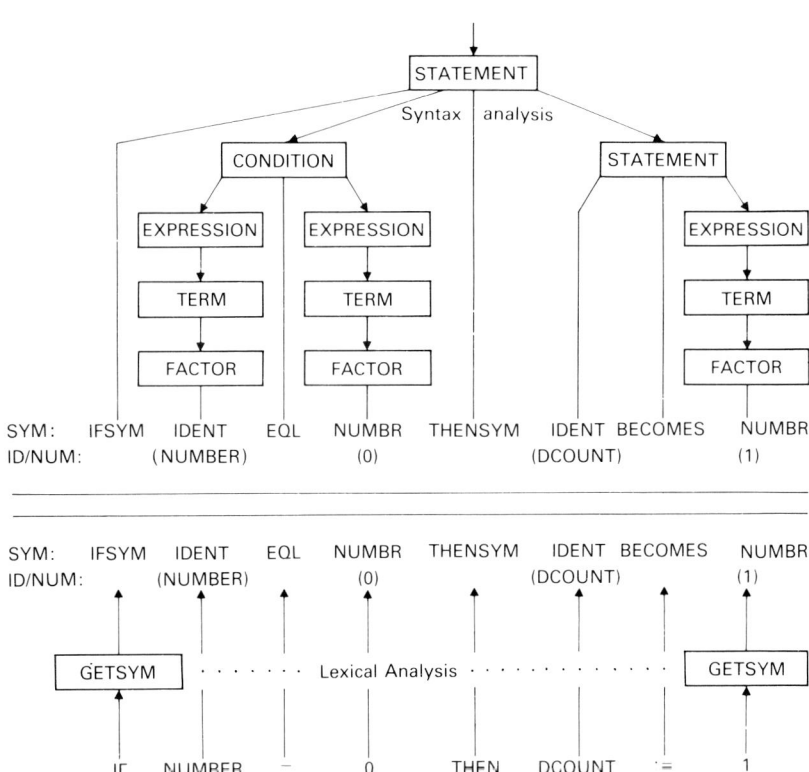

Fig. 3.2a. Lexical and syntax analysis of a sample IF statement.

Syntax analysis/code synthesis

The second phase, syntax analysis with code synthesis, is the fulcrum of the compiler. It is here that syntactic structure is ascertained, i.e. the constituent grammatical constructions of the source program such as terms, factors, expressions, declarations, complete statements and the program block are recognized, and equivalent sequences of target program instructions are immediately composed for each source construct concerned. Thus syntax

Chapter 3

analysis and code synthesis proceed hand in hand. (In the two syntax checkers,
PARSER0 and PARSER, the purpose of syntax analysis is solely to verify source
program grammatical correctness, so no target code is produced at all. The
reasons for having both these programs and a separate compiler in the PL/T
system are, firstly, that PARSER0 is deliberately simplified for use in an
introductory source code study context, leaving PARSER and COMPILXEC as
production tools for source program syntax checking and translation,
respectively; and secondly, that role specialization of the latter two programs
makes them smaller in execution size and easier to study individually.
Separation of syntax checking and translation functions in this way can also be
said, arguably, to correspond most usefully to the way in which student
programs are typically developed.)

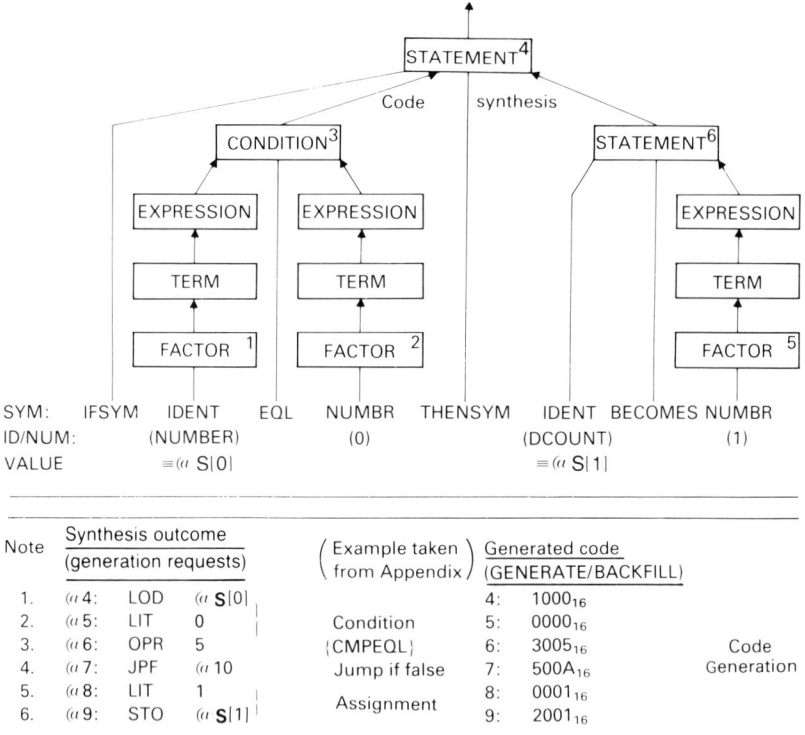

Fig. 3.2b. Code synthesis and generation for sample IF statement.

The background information required for understanding this phase of COMPILXEC in more detail is given in Chapter 6 (source language syntax), Chapter 7 (target machine definition) and Chapter 8 (source/target language correspondence). A supporting illustration showing the translation of a sample statement is presented in Figures 3.2a (lexical/syntax analysis) and 3.2b (code synthesis/generation). From a source text comprehension viewpoint, the most significant characteristic of COMPILXEC is the way in which the structure of its syntax analysis/code synthesis part follows directly from Chapter 6: every PL/T syntactic entity has an associated Pascal procedure and the language-defining operations each map naturally into Pascal programming constructs—(implicit) succession into sequence (BEGIN. . .END), alternation/optionality into selection (IF), repeatable optionality into conditional repetition (WHILE) and subordination (reference to a subordinate entity definition) into procedure invocation (by entity name).

Thus, for example, the procedure EXPRESSION (see page 46), whose job is to process an arithmetic expression, allows first for the possibility of an optional + or − sign (using IF), then calls TERM to deal with the compulsory initial term of the expression, then makes allowance for optional further terms (using WHILE). This basic grammatical correspondence applies in the same way to all the other relevant procedures and is complicated only by the interspersion of code synthesis and obvious error checking actions (the lexical analyser is called upon also, to provide the next source symbol each time processing of the current one is completed).

Description of this central phase of compiler activity is completed by considering the role of the supporting identifier table, which is used to record the names and values of all user-defined constant and variable identifiers pertaining to a PL/T source program. This table (IDTABLE) is built during processing of constant and variable declarations by entering the name and kind of each identifier declared together with a corresponding numeric or address target value, respectively. The information recorded is then available for reference during subsequent compilation of the imperative program—specifically, expressions and assignment statements. It is used both in syntax analysis, where name and kind details enable detection of errors such as the occurrence of an undeclared identifier or an attempt to assign to a constant, and in code synthesis, where the kind and value of an identifier is obviously relevant, e.g. in constructing and choosing between a LIT or LOD instruction (cf. Chapter 8). Identifier table look-up is achieved by simple linear searching.

Code generation

The third and final phase of COMPILXEC is code generation, the fabrication and output of actual target machine instructions (16-bit words) from the function codes and argument values provided as results of code synthesis. This is illustrated in Figure 3.2b (lower half). In the case of the PL/T target machine there is only one instruction format so generation (GENERATE) is very easy: each function code (4 bits) and argument value (12 bits) pair are simply packed together and deposited in the next available target program store location (see Chapter 7 for details). The only complication to this arrangement is caused by forward jump instructions—instructions whose destination address argument is not yet known when they are generated and has to be filled in later. This 'forward reference' problem is demonstrated in Chapter 8 and solved cooperatively between code synthesis and code generation phases (by STATEMENT and BACKFILL, respectively).

In summary, COMPILXEC is a complete illustration, in simple form, of the entire compilation process. The key to understanding it is to recognize its structure in terms of phases and modules as described above. These can then be studied individually in detail and the whole comprehended as the sum of its parts.

Chapter 4

Overview of Machine Interpreter Program

The purpose of the PL/T interpreter (INTERPRET) is to execute PL/T machine language programs in the main store (MEMORY) of the PL/T 'machine' following their direct generation into that store by the PL/T compiler. In the absence of a real, hardware, equivalent this is done by simulating each part of the machine—store, CPU and registers—in software form. The complete context for this simulation is described in detail in Chapter 7 (target machine definition), which is taken as read in what follows. Physically, INTERPRET is a subprogram of COMPILXEC (cf. Figure 3.1), hence the relevant source listing material includes the main program and supervisory routine sections of the latter, from which calls on INTERPRET actually originate.

As a program, the interpreter itself is very much smaller and simpler than its companion compiler. It consists simply of an initialization section which sets the three PL/T store addressing registers (PP, SB, SP) to their correct starting values and all variables to a suitably distinctive 'undefined' initial value (-32767), followed by a main loop which implements the standard fetch−decode−execute instruction processing cycle of the machine's CPU. The execute part of this loop consists of an indexed selection from the function repertoire of the CPU, extended by secondary (sub-function) indexing in the case of the OPR function. Instruction processing continues until a halt state obtains, either normally, as a result of a halt (HLT) instruction, or abnormally, due to the occurrence of an execution error (stack overflow or division by zero).

A brief output trace, in source language terms, of each variable assignment is always produced, and this may be augmented at the user's behest by a full or partial execution trace showing the contents of the main processor registers and current top-of-stack locations on a per-instruction basis. If successful, interpretation always concludes with a source level listing of the final values of all the variables declared in the user's program so that results are visible (in lieu of direct output). This summary is produced by a separate controlling routine (EXECUTE) which is also responsible for determining the user's execution trace requirements initially, prior to invoking the interpreter proper.

Like many similar programs, the interpreter has to strike a balance between realism and reasonable efficiency. Thus it does not check for illegal function codes, on the assumption that the compiler should not generate these, or for arithmetic overflow, which it leaves for the underlying Pascal system to catch. In addition, although it does initialize all variables to 'undefined', it does not check subsequent attempts to use variables that are still in that state. On the positive side, however, the availability of detailed execution tracing makes it possible for all these errors to be tracked down without much difficulty should they arise. On balance, therefore, efficiency is achieved without loss of effectiveness.

Chapter 5

PL/T Source Language:
Lexical (Vocabulary) Definition

The alphabet of the PL/T source language comprises the upper case letters, the decimal digits and the characters $+ - * / ( ) < = > : ; \{ \}$, . space and end-of-line. Within comments only, these may be augmented by any other characters from the character set of the computer system being used. This alphabet is used to form the following vocabulary of basic language symbols:

Reserved words	CONST, VAR
	used in named-constant definition and variable declaration, respectively;
	BEGIN, END, IF, THEN, WHILE, DO
	used in the normal way, cf. Pascal
Identifiers	User-defined constant and variable names consisting of an initial letter, possibly followed by additional letters or digits; the first eight characters only are taken to be significant in determining identifier uniqueness. Identifiers must be distinct from the reserved words of the language
Integer numbers	Unsigned decimal numbers in the range 0 to 32767. This range is reduced to an effective range of 0 to 4095 in the implementation of PL/T described in this handbook (as explained in Chapter 7)
Assignment and arithmetic operators, and brackets	$+ - * / ( ) :=$ used in integer arithmetic calculations only (thus / indicates integer division)
Logical (Boolean) comparison operators	$= <> < <= > >=$ used in building IF and WHILE conditions

Punctuation symbols   ;   used to separate (*not terminate*) source statements
                          .   used to terminate source programs
                          ,   used to separate constant definitions and variable declarations

                          { } used to enclose commentary

                          space(s): used to delimit reserved words where required, and for normal source text presentation purposes

                          end-of-line: equivalent to space

Note: Since source program input to the PL/T system is by means of files prepared in advance using host computer-resident software facilities, input editing operations involving characters such as backspace and delete are assumed to have been completed beforehand (during source file creation) and therefore to have no lexical significance.

Chapter 6

PL/T Source Language: Syntactic (Grammatical) Definition

PL/T source language grammar is defined below in two alternative forms: by syntax diagrams, and in equivalent but more concise Extended Backus Naur Form (EBNF). The special language definition metasymbols of the latter notation are ::= indicating definition, | for alternation, [ ] for optionality, { } for repeatable optionality, ( ) for grouping and < > to distinguish syntactic entities; the notation also makes implicit use of succession and subordination operations. Identifiers and (unsigned) numbers are treated as basic symbols for purposes of syntax definition; other basic symbols, from the source language vocabulary, stand for themselves.

EBNF: <Program> ::=<Block>.

(In English this would be written as:
'A Program is defined to be a Block followed by a full stop').

<Block> ::= [CONST <Constdeclaration> {, <Constdeclaration>} ;]
           VAR <Vardeclaration> {, <Vardeclaration>} ; <Statement>

<Constdeclaration> ::= identifier = number

<Vardeclaration> ::= identifier

<Statement> ::= identifier := <Expression> |
               IF <Condition> THEN <Statement> |
               BEGIN <Statement> {; <Statement>} END |
               WHILE <Condition> DO <Statement>

<Condition> ::= <Expression> (=|< >|<|<=|>|>=) <Expression>

<Expression> ::= [(+|−)] <Term> {(+|−) <Term>}

<Term> ::= <Factor> {(*|/)<Factor>}

<Factor> ::= identifier |number | (<Expression>)

(In English this would be written as:
'A Factor is defined to be either an identifier, or a number, or a left bracket followed by an Expression followed by a right bracket').

Chapter 6

Note: As discussed in Chapter 3, the complete language grammar may be converted directly into an equivalent recognition program by associating a procedure with each syntactic entity and mapping the definitional operations of succession, alternation/optionality, repeatable optionality and subordination into sequence (BEGIN. . .END), selection (IF), conditional repetition (WHILE) and delegation (procedure call) programming constructs, respectively.

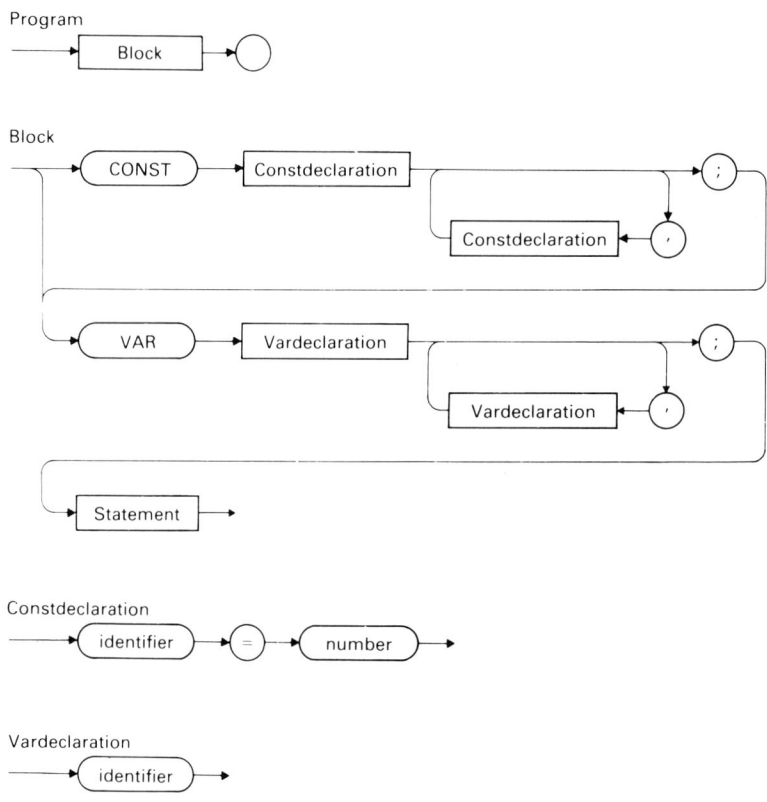

PL/T Syntax Diagrams. Program, Block, Constdeclaration, Vardeclaration.

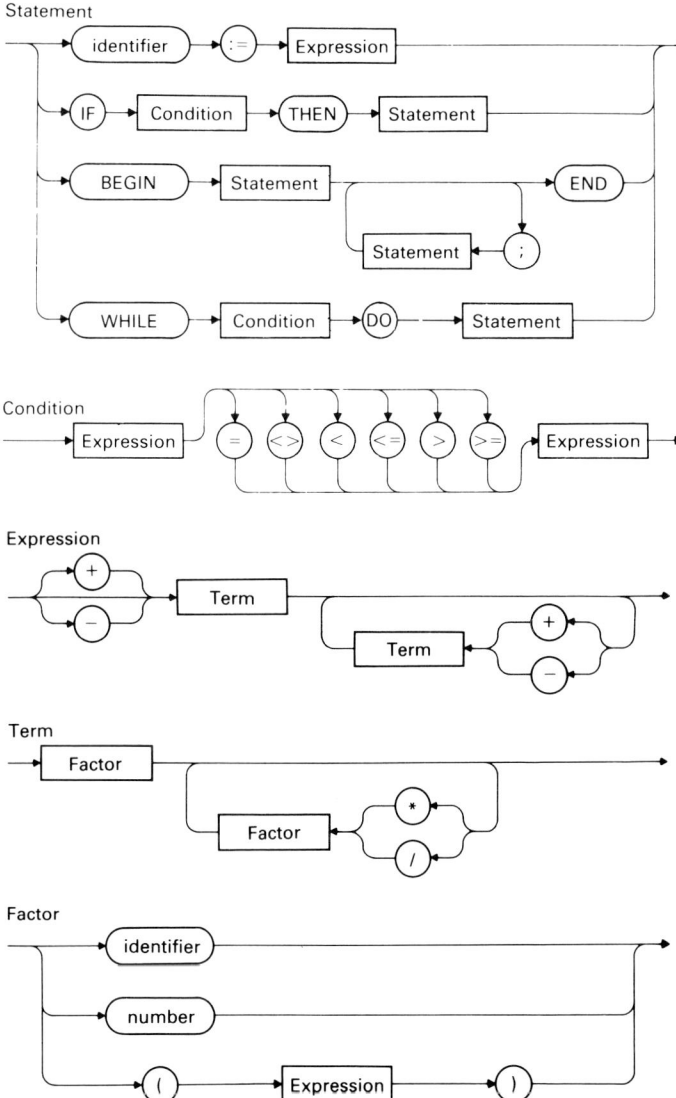

PL/T Syntax Diagrams. Statement, Condition, Expression, Term, Factor.

Chapter 7

PL/T 'Machine': Definition

At the start of this handbook we indicated that the reason for using a hypothetical target computer for PL/T was that this target could be specifically designed to make compilation relatively easy. This objective is achieved by devising a package of 'hardware' facilities which, together, match the available source language constructs and overall source program limitations as closely as possible (and exclusively), thus providing a highly constrained, near-ideal context in which translation can take place. Chapter 2 contains a perfect example of the kind of source program to be supported in this way. Having done this, the second major design consideration is that the target machine should be easy to implement by interpreter on real computers— particularly, in the case of PL/T, 16-bit word microcomputers with possibly limited primary storage.

Overall, the PL/T 'computer' is consequently an extremely simple machine consisting of a CPU with minimal control and arithmetic/logic capabilities, a 1K only 16-bit word main store (called MEMORY) and no direct input/output! It has only five registers altogether: a 16-bit current instruction register (IR), three 10-bit registers for program instruction addressing (PP) and variable addressing (SB, SP), and a 1-bit CPU status flag (CPUSTATE). Instruction execution, using PP and IR, follows normal sequential practice but excludes any subroutining capability. The most distinctive characteristic of the machine, as we shall see, is that all calculation is based on a concise workspace *stack* mechanism; hence there is no need for any accumulator registers, as such, in the architecture. Signed, 16-bit integers are the sole data type supported. However, despite all these limitations and simplifications, this carefully chosen combination of elements is entirely adequate for the purposes we have defined, as will now be demonstrated.

Storage architecture

The PL/T compiler utilizes these facilities by placing target program instructions at the bottom of store, from location 0 upwards, and allocating room for variables in whatever space is left (again working upwards, one word per variable). As the start address of the latter store area depends on the size of the program concerned and this is not known at the time of compiling variable declarations, all variables are given addresses that are *relative* to an implicit execution register (SB), which is set to the base address of the variables' store area during interpreter initialization (by which time it is known). Thus the actual (absolute) store address of each variable at execution time is given by its relative address + SB.

This basing convention also extends to anonymous, calculation workspace 'variables', which are created and discarded dynamically as necessary during execution in the store area immediately above that reserved for the permanent (explicit) variables. The machine model requires calculation to be organized so that this area is always allocated and used in a particular way, namely that all the operand values for each given operation should be created (loaded or calculated) one at a time in order, before then being replaced *en bloc* by their corresponding result. Consequently the workspace area as a whole operates as a stack, with all activity definable in terms of the latest, 'top', entry position. This position is indicated by SP, the (SB-relative) top-of-stack pointer register, which is initially set to point to the high end of the permanent variables' store area and is increased by 1 before entering a value onto the stack and decreased by 1 after removing a value from it. Because they share the same base address and the difference between them is clear, it is convenient in practice to drop the distinction between permanent and workspace variables and to consider the two groups together as a single concatenated stack structure in which the permanent variables are included as a fixed initial section. SB is then the common stack base register.

The above description of main store operational layout is summarized in Figure 7.1 and illustrated in the following example.

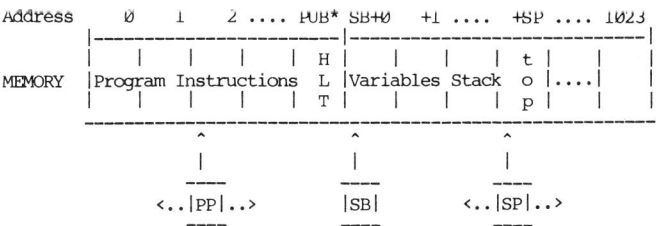

Fig. 7.1. PL/T machine store illustration. (*PUB = Program Upper Bound.)

Example

In the sample, digit counting program used throughout this handbook (see Appendix), PUB is 23, SB is therefore 24, the two declared variables have relative stack positions 0 and 1, and two further stack locations, 2 and 3, are used anonymously during program execution. SP, the (SB-relative) top-of-stack pointer, oscillates between 1 and 3 as calculation workspace requirements vary. PP, the program pointer, starts at 0 and (eventually) terminates at 24 (PUB+1) on execution of the final program instruction (HLT).

Function set and associated instruction formats

Following on from the general model defined above, the function repertoire of the PL/T machine consists of orders to load literal (LIT) and variable (LOD) values onto the top of the stack for use in calculation, to store/remove (STO) a calculation result from the top of the stack into a variable, to operate on values at the top of the stack (OPR), to transfer control unconditionally (JMP) or conditionally (JPF), and to terminate execution (HLT). The OPR function is always qualified by a specific arithmetic or logical sub-function, to be applied to a single value or pair of values as appropriate and giving a single result value in their place. Sub-functions available include negation (NEG), addition (ADD) and subtraction (SUB), multiplication (MPY) and division (DVD), and a complete set of comparison (CMP) tests, which produce a true (1) or false (0) result on the top of the stack ready for immediate use (and removal) by a following JPF (Jump if False) conditional transfer instruction. All non-control functions and sub-functions take integer operands and (comparisons apart) produce 16-bit integer results.

A small selection of the functions available is illustrated in Figure 7.2 below by means of a machine language program fragment, suitably annotated, from the digit counting program. Here every instruction is shown in both 4-digit hexadecimal and decoded symbolic representations and the two variables involved, NUMBER and DCOUNT, have relative stack addresses 0 and 1, respectively. OPR sub-function 5 is equality comparison (CMPEQL) and the stack is symbolically referred to as S.

```
{IF NUMBER=0 THEN DCOUNT:=1}

@4: (#1000#)   LOD  @S[0]   Load from NUMBER onto top of Stack
@5: (#0000#)   LIT  0       Load 0 onto top of Stack
@6: (#3005#)   OPR  5       Compare top two Stack values for equality
@7: (#500A#)   JPF  @10     Jump if CMPEQL result False to address 10
@8: (#0001#)   LIT  1       Load 1 onto top of Stack
@9: (#2001#)   STO  @S[1]   Store from top of Stack into DCOUNT
```

Fig. 7.2. PL/T machine language program fragment.

All PL/T machine language instructions are the same size, one 16-bit word long, with the leading (most significant) 4 bits representing the function code number of each (underlined in Figure 7.2). This leaves 12 bits for a single instruction argument field representing as appropriate an absolute instruction address or SB-relative variable address, a positive numeric literal value, or an OPR sub-function code number. Since the only way in which numeric literals can be generated in PL/T machine language is by means of the LIT instruction this reduces the effective range of such values to 0 through 4095. Otherwise, for addresses and sub-function codes, 12 bits is more than adequate. In the latter case it may surprise the reader to learn that both fields of an OPR instruction are taken up in specifying the operation concerned, without apparent reference to any associated operand(s), i.e. OPR is a '0-address' instruction. The reason for this is that the necessary operand(s) (and their result) are addressed *implicitly* via SP, the top-of-stack pointer register; hence, explicit addressing is unnecessary.

Chapter 8

PL/T Source/Machine Language Correspondence

Having considered, in the preceding three chapters, definitions of the PL/T source language and target machine, we are in a position here to establish their correspondence, that is to define a suitable translation of each source language construct into machine language instructions. Together with the companion chapters, this completes the prerequisite context for understanding the architecture of the PL/T system programs.

Constant and variable declarations

These do not of themselves have any associated machine code, instead they provide information about identifiers which is essential to the translation of expressions and assignments subsequently. The relevant information for each declared identifier comprises name, type and target value details, where the value of a constant identifier is that of the number for which it stands and the value of a variable identifier is the corresponding relative stack position (0 for the first variable declared, 1 for the second, and so on) as previously discussed.

Expressions and assignments

The basic *modus operandi* of stack-based calculation means that all the operand values relevant to an operation must be present in order at the top of the stack before the operation can take place. In translation terms this requirement may be met by implicitly reordering infix source expressions into postfix (also called 'reverse Polish') form and immediately generating a LIT or LOD instruction as appropriate for each constant or variable operand, respectively, prior to generating the relevant OPR instruction. Thus in the supplied sample program, the infix expression NUMBER / RADIX becomes NUMBER RADIX / (postfix), resulting in the production of the three instructions

LOD @S[0], LIT 10, OPR 4 {DVD}

When executed this instruction sequence will load first the current value of NUMBER, then the value 10 (RADIX) onto the top of the stack, before dividing the former by the latter and replacing the pair by their single result.

The above strategy generalizes without alteration to the translation of arbitrarily complex arithmetic expressions and also the simple Boolean expressions employed in conditional control contexts. Assignment statements are then handled by remembering the name of the destination variable concerned when it occurs and generating an STO instruction for that variable immediately following the code generated for the associated assignment expression. Within expressions the corresponding source language syntax, directly applied, automatically ensures that normal operator precedence priorities will be correctly reproduced.

Control statements

Apart from the generation of a halt (HLT) instruction marking the end of a complete source program, there are only two other source constructs, the IF and WHILE statements, for which machine language needs to be produced. Both of these statements are governed by a controlling condition which, we have seen, translates into machine instructions whose execution effect is to leave a Boolean result value—false (0) or true (1)—on top of the stack. The appropriate translation action for both IF and WHILE is to generate a conditional jump (JPF) immediately following this instruction sequence, which will skip over the code for the associated consequent source statement at execution time if the condition result on the stack is false (and remove it whether false or true). In the case of WHILE, a further, unconditional jump (JMP) instruction is also required, following the code for the consequent statement, to close the WHILE loop. The complete machine language patterns for the two statements are therefore as shown in Figure 8.1 (once again a specific example of each can be found in the Appendix).

```
{IF Condition THEN Statement}    {WHILE Condition DO Statement}

machine code for Condition       LOOP: machine code for Condition
     JPF   NEXT                        JPF   NEXT
machine code for Statement             machine code for Statement
NEXT: ...   ....                       JMP   LOOP
                                 NEXT:       ...   ....
```

Fig. 8.1. Machine code templates for IF and WHILE constructs.

Note: The reader will observe that in both cases the JPF instruction is a forward jump, i.e. its destination address (NEXT) is not yet known at the time when the instruction is generated. The answer to this 'forward reference' problem is to arrange for the missing details to be filled in later, once they become known. This problem does not, of course, arise with backward jumps.

Chapter 9

PL/T Software System Release: Summary

At the time of writing, this release consists of three system programs written in the TURBO dialect of Pascal—a 'sudden death' syntax checker, an error-recovering syntax checker, and a combined compiler/machine interpreter program—together with one sample PL/T test program. The system programs are supplied in both executable and source form, distinguished as Code and Text files, respectively, in the conventional way. All three programs, when operating, take PL/T source input from a user-specified file, which is assumed to have been prepared in advance using the facilities of the host computer's resident software system. Output is to the user's terminal and, if requested, to an equivalent named copy file on disc. A brief summary of each program is given below. Detailed instructions on program usage are provided in the companion Chapter 10.

PARSER0 (.PAS and .COM files)

A 'sudden death' syntax checker, so-called because it does not attempt to recover when a user source program error is detected, but simply terminates instead (after indicating the error). Intended primarily for source code study purposes, e.g. as an initial exercise preceding study of COMPILXEC, which is larger and more complex.

PARSER (.PAS and .COM files)

A 'persistent' syntax checker which does try (within reason) to recover its composure and continue operating after detecting source errors. Not suitable for source code study by introductory course students, but essential for use in the development of PL/T source programs that are syntactically correct *since this is assumed by COMPILXEC*. Provides per-line error explanations and file copy output as user-selectable options.

COMPILXEC (.PAS and .COM files)
(uses PRINTS, GETSYM and INTERP .PAS files)

This program compiles, then immediately executes, syntactically correct
PL/T user programs. Various forms of generated code and execution trace
displays, as well as file copy output, may be selected by the user. Suitable for
source code study, particularly as it builds directly on PARSER0 by refinement
thereof.

The PL/T machine interpreter, as part of COMPILXEC, is contained in the
inclusion file INTERP.PAS.

SAMPLE (.PLT file)

A program to count how many digits a number contains. This program is
carefully devised to provide a comprehensive illustration of the PL/T language
and PL/T system operation as concisely as possible.

Chapter 10

Using the PL/T Programming System under TURBO Pascal

This chapter complements the previous one by showing in detail how the component tools of the PL/T system are actually applied to the development of user programs. For this purpose the development cycle as a whole is considered as consisting of three distinct sequential steps:

(i) program creation/alteration, using a suitable Editor;
(ii) program syntax correctness checking, using PARSER;
(iii) program compilation and immediate execution, using COMPILXEC.

Each of these steps is described below in the context of a TURBO Pascal host software system, taking the sample test program SAMPLE.PLT from the PL/T software release as a development example. User responses to system prompt messages are distinguished throughout by underlining and are completed by typing end-of-line in each case; end-of-line on its own is an acceptable negative response abbreviation. Selection prompts are illustrated by showing the response which is likely to be most appropriate in the normal student program development situation. Possible alternative responses are summarized separately in note form.

PL/T program creation/alteration

In the assumed context this may be accomplished by means of the standard TURBO-resident Editor. The program files thus produced must be distinguished as PL/T files by a .PLT suffix. SAMPLE.PLT is a ready-made example.

PL/T program syntax checking

This is achieved by executing the Code file PARSER.COM, viz:

X PARSER

with the following recommended dialogue:

```
PLEASE TYPE IN NAME OF PL/T SOURCE CODE TEXT FILE: SAMPLE
PLEASE TYPE IN NAME OF OUTPUT LIST FILE ("RETURN" FOR NONE): SAMPLE

DO YOU WANT ERROR MESSAGES (BESIDES NUMBERS) AFTER EACH LINE?
ANSWER Y(ES) IF YOU DO, OTHERWISE NO WILL BE ASSUMED: Y
```

The above sequence takes source program input from the file SAMPLE.PLT and produces a check listing with error indications (if any) on the user's terminal and in the file SAMPLE.LST. The latter file is available for inspection and (if required) printing thereafter. Per-line error explanations are recommended as an aid to inspecting PARSER output on screen-based terminal devices, but are not essential, as a cumulative error message summary is always provided, independently, at the end of the check listing. A negative response to the prompt concerned would reduce the volume of output generated for erroneous programs.

PL/T program compilation and execution

This is achieved by executing the Code file COMPILXE. COM,viz:

X COMPILXE

with the following recommended dialogue:

```
PLEASE TYPE IN NAME OF PL/T SOURCE CODE TEXT FILE: SAMPLE
PLEASE TYPE IN NAME OF OUTPUT LIST FILE ("RETURN" FOR NONE): SAMPLE

DO YOU WANT A MACHINE CODE LISTING AFTER EACH SOURCE LINE?
ANSWER Y(ES) IF YOU DO, OTHERWISE NO WILL BE ASSUMED: N

DO YOU WANT A TRACE, FULL OR PARTIAL, OF PROGRAM EXECUTION?
ANSWER F(ULL) OR P(ARTIAL), OTHERWISE NONE WILL BE ASSUMED: N
```

The above sequence takes source program input from the file SAMPLE.PLT and produces compilation and execution result listings in turn on the user's terminal and in the file SAMPLE.LST. This file is again available for inspection and printing thereafter. The compilation and execution listings produced automatically include a cumulative generated machine code summary and variable assignment trace/final value summary, respectively. Per-line machine code and more extensive, per-instruction, trace listing options should only be needed in illustrative and exceptional debugging circumstances. If required, execution tracing in particular should be used with great care, otherwise unnecessarily excessive amounts of output can easily result.

Chapter 11

PARSER0
System Program Listing

```
(*$A-*)
PROGRAM PARSER0;                {PL/T: SYNTAX CHECKING WITHOUT ERROR RECOVERY}

{!!!! DATA DEFINITIONS !!!!}

CONST IDENTMAXSIZE = 8;      {MAX. SIGNIFICANT LENGTH OF IDENTIFIERS}
      NUMBRMAXSIZE = 5;      {MAX. NO. OF DIGITS IN NUMBERS}
      MAXIMUMNUMBR = 32767;  {MAX. NUMERICAL VALUE}
      MAXCHARCODE  = 255;    {MAX. CHARACTER CODE VALUE}
      MAXLINESIZE  = 255;    {MAX. SOURCE LINE LENGTH}
      NOOFRESWRDS  = 8;      {NO. OF PL/T RESERVED WORDS}
      RESWRDLIMIT  = 9;      {MAX. BOUND ON RESERVED WORD SEARCH}
      IDTABMAXSIZE = 50;     {MAX. SIZE OF IDENTIFIER TABLE}
      NOOFERRMESGS = 27;     {NO. OF ERROR MESSAGES}
      NULLFILENAME = '!PLTNULL';    {NAME OF NULL OUTPUT FILE}

TYPE  IDSTRING = STRING[IDENTMAXSIZE];       {IDENTIFIER CHARACTER STRING}
      IDKIND   = (CONSTANT,VARIABLE);        {POSSIBLE KINDS OF IDENTIFIER}
      NUMBRVALUE = 0..MAXIMUMNUMBR;          {UNSIGNED NUMERICAL VALUE}
      RESWRDNUMBER = 1..NOOFRESWRDS;         {RESERVED WORD NUMBER}
      IDENTNUMBER  = 0..IDTABMAXSIZE;        {IDENTIFIER TABLE ENTRY NUMBER}
      ERRORNUMBER  = 1..NOOFERRMESGS;        {ERROR/ERROR MESSAGE NUMBER}
      MESSAGETEXT  = STRING[80];             {ERROR/OTHER MESSAGE TEXT}

      {POSSIBLE KINDS OF SYMBOL, I.E. LEXICAL TOKENS}
      SYMBOL    = (NUL, IDENT, NUMBR, PLUS, MINUS, TIMES, SLASH,
                   EQL, NEQ, LSS, LEQ, GTR, GEQ, BECOMES,
                   LPAREN, RPAREN, COMMA, SEMICOLON, PERIOD,
                   CONSTSYM, VARSYM, BEGINSYM, ENDSYM,
                   IFSYM, THENSYM, WHILESYM, DOSYM);

VAR   SOURCEFILE, OUTPUTFILE: TEXT;         {SOURCE AND OUTPUT FILES}
      SOURCENAME, OUTPUTNAME: STRING[20];   {SOURCE AND OUTPUT FILE NAMES}

      SOURCELINE: STRING[MAXLINESIZE];      {CURRENT SOURCE LINE}
      LINELENGTH: 0..MAXLINESIZE;           {LENGTH OF CURRENT SOURCE LINE}
      LINEPTR: 0..MAXLINESIZE;              {CURRENT POSITION WITHIN SOURCE LINE}

      CH: CHAR;             {MOST RECENTLY RECOGNISED CHARACTER}
      SYM: SYMBOL;          {MOST RECENTLY RECOGNISED SYMBOL}
      ID: IDSTRING;         {MOST RECENTLY RECOGNISED IDENTIFIER}
      NUM: NUMBRVALUE;      {MOST RECENTLY RECOGNISED NUMBER}

      CHARSYMS: ARRAY[CHAR] OF SYMBOL;      {SYMBOLS FOR INDIVIDUAL CHARACTERS}

      RESWRDS: ARRAY[RESWRDNUMBER] OF IDSTRING;    {RESERVED WORD LIST}
      RESWRDSYMS: ARRAY[RESWRDNUMBER] OF SYMBOL;   {SYMBOLS FOR RESERVED WORDS}

      IDTABLE: ARRAY[IDENTNUMBER] OF        {IDENTIFIER TABLE}
               RECORD NAME: IDSTRING;       {IDENTIFIER NAME}
                      KIND: IDKIND          {IDENTIFIER KIND}
               END;
      IDCOUNT: IDENTNUMBER;                 {IDENTIFIER TABLE ENTRY COUNT}

      ERRMESGS: ARRAY[ERRORNUMBER] OF MESSAGETEXT; {ERROR MESSAGE LIST}
```

30

```
{!!!! INITIALISATION AND PRINTOUT ROUTINES !!!!}

PROCEDURE INITIALISE;                    {INITIALISES GLOBAL VARIABLES}

   PROCEDURE INITSYMBOLS;                {INITIALISES CHARSYMS AND RESWRDS/SYMS}

   VAR   ICH: CHAR;

   BEGIN {INITIALISE SYMBOLS FOR INDIVIDUAL CHARACTERS}
         FOR ICH:=CHR(0) TO CHR(MAXCHARCODE) DO CHARSYMS[ICH]:=NUL;
         CHARSYMS['+']:=PLUS;  CHARSYMS['-']:=MINUS;      CHARSYMS['*']:=TIMES;
         CHARSYMS['/']:=SLASH; CHARSYMS['(']:=LPAREN;     CHARSYMS[')']:=RPAREN;
         CHARSYMS['=']:=EQL;   CHARSYMS['<']:=LSS;        CHARSYMS['>']:=GTR;
         CHARSYMS[',']:=COMMA; CHARSYMS[';']:=SEMICOLON;  CHARSYMS['.']:=PERIOD;

         {INITIALISE RESERVED WORD AND ASSOCIATED SYMBOL LISTS, ALPHABETICALLY}
         RESWRDS[1]:='BEGIN   ';     RESWRDSYMS[1]:=BEGINSYM;
         RESWRDS[2]:='CONST   ';     RESWRDSYMS[2]:=CONSTSYM;
         RESWRDS[3]:='DO      ';     RESWRDSYMS[3]:=DOSYM;
         RESWRDS[4]:='END     ';     RESWRDSYMS[4]:=ENDSYM;
         RESWRDS[5]:='IF      ';     RESWRDSYMS[5]:=IFSYM;
         RESWRDS[6]:='THEN    ';     RESWRDSYMS[6]:=THENSYM;
         RESWRDS[7]:='VAR     ';     RESWRDSYMS[7]:=VARSYM;
         RESWRDS[8]:='WHILE   ';     RESWRDSYMS[8]:=WHILESYM
   END {INITSYMBOLS};

   PROCEDURE INITERRMESGS;              {INITIALISES ERROR MESSAGE LIST}
   BEGIN ERRMESGS[1] :='"VAR" DECLARATION(S) EXPECTED.';
         ERRMESGS[2] :='"=" MUST BE FOLLOWED BY A NUMBER.';
         ERRMESGS[3] :='IDENTIFIER MUST BE FOLLOWED BY "=".';
         ERRMESGS[4] :='"CONST" OR "VAR" MUST BE FOLLOWED BY AN IDENTIFIER.';
         ERRMESGS[5] :='SEMICOLON OR COMMA MISSING.';
         ERRMESGS[6] :='SYSTEM FAULT - PLEASE REPORT TO TUTOR.';
         ERRMESGS[7] :='STATEMENT EXPECTED.';
         ERRMESGS[8] :=ERRMESGS[6];
         ERRMESGS[9] :='FULL STOP EXPECTED.';
         ERRMESGS[10]:=ERRMESGS[6];
         ERRMESGS[11]:='UNDECLARED IDENTIFIER.';
         ERRMESGS[12]:='ASSIGNMENT TO CONSTANT IS NOT ALLOWED.';
         ERRMESGS[13]:='ASSIGNMENT OPERATOR ":=" EXPECTED.';
         ERRMESGS[14]:=ERRMESGS[6];
         ERRMESGS[15]:=ERRMESGS[6];
         ERRMESGS[16]:='"THEN" EXPECTED.';
         ERRMESGS[17]:='SEMICOLON OR "END" EXPECTED.';
         ERRMESGS[18]:='"DO" EXPECTED.';
         ERRMESGS[19]:=ERRMESGS[6];
         ERRMESGS[20]:='RELATIONAL OPERATOR EXPECTED.';
         ERRMESGS[21]:=ERRMESGS[6];
         ERRMESGS[22]:='RIGHT PARENTHESIS MISSING.';
         ERRMESGS[23]:='IDENTIFIER, NUMBER OR "(" EXPECTED.';
         ERRMESGS[24]:=ERRMESGS[6];
         ERRMESGS[25]:='NUMBER TOO LARGE.';
         ERRMESGS[26]:='IDENTIFIER TABLE OVERFLOW.';
         ERRMESGS[27]:='SOURCE PROGRAM INCOMPLETE.'
   END {INITERRMESGS};
```

```
BEGIN {INITIALISE SYMBOLS, IDENTIFIER TABLE AND ERROR MESSAGE LIST}
     INITSYMBOLS;           IDCOUNT:=0;           INITERRMESGS;
     {INITIALISE LEXICAL STATE VARIABLES}
     LINELENGTH:=0; LINEPTR:=0; CH:=' '
END {INITIALISE};

PROCEDURE PRINTLN(MESG: MESSAGETEXT); {WRITES MESSAGE LINE TO SCREEN AND FILE}
BEGIN WRITELN(MESG); WRITELN(OUTPUTFILE,MESG)
END {PRINTLN};

PROCEDURE PRINTNL;                     {WRITES BLANK LINE TO SCREEN AND FILE}
BEGIN WRITELN; WRITELN(OUTPUTFILE)
END {PRINTNL};

PROCEDURE PRINTERROR(EN: ERRORNUMBER); {WRITES "POSITIONAL" ERROR MESSAGE TO
                                  SCREEN AND FILE, THEN ABORTS PARSING}
BEGIN WRITELN(' ':LINEPTR,'^',EN:1); WRITELN(EN:2,': ',ERRMESGS[EN]);
     WRITELN(OUTPUTFILE,' ':LINEPTR,'^',EN:1);
     WRITELN(OUTPUTFILE,EN:2,': ',ERRMESGS[EN]);

     CLOSE(SOURCEFILE);

     PRINTNL; PRINTNL;
     PRINTLN('^^^^^^^^^^^^^^^^^^^^^^^^^^^^^^^^');
     PRINTLN('^ SYNTAX CHECKING ABORTED. ^');
     PRINTLN('^^^^^^^^^^^^^^^^^^^^^^^^^^^^^^^^');
     PRINTNL; PRINTNL;

     CLOSE(OUTPUTFILE);
     IF OUTPUTNAME = NULLFILENAME THEN ERASE(OUTPUTFILE)
     ELSE WRITELN('(SEE ',CONCAT(OUTPUTNAME,'.LST'),' FOR OUTPUT.)');
     WRITELN;

     HALT
END {PRINTERROR};

PROCEDURE PRINTABORT(EN: ERRORNUMBER); {WRITES "DISASTROUS" ERROR MESSAGE TO
                                  SCREEN AND FILE, THEN ABORTS PARSING}
BEGIN PRINTNL; PRINTLN(ERRMESGS[EN]);

     CLOSE(SOURCEFILE);

     PRINTNL; PRINTNL;
     PRINTLN('^^^^^^^^^^^^^^^^^^^^^^^^^^^^^^^^');
     PRINTLN('^ SYNTAX CHECKING ABORTED. ^');
     PRINTLN('^^^^^^^^^^^^^^^^^^^^^^^^^^^^^^^^');
     PRINTNL; PRINTNL;

     CLOSE(OUTPUTFILE);
     IF OUTPUTNAME = NULLFILENAME THEN ERASE(OUTPUTFILE)
     ELSE WRITELN('(SEE ',CONCAT(OUTPUTNAME,'.LST'),' FOR OUTPUT.)');
     WRITELN;

     HALT
END {PRINTABORT};
```

```
{!!!! LEXICAL ANALYSIS (SYMBOL RECOGNITION) ROUTINES !!!!}

PROCEDURE GETSYM;                        {GETS NEXT SOURCE PROGRAM SYMBOL}

VAR   SIZE: 0..MAXLINESIZE; LOWER, MIDDLE, UPPER: 0..RESWRDLIMIT; DIGIT: 0..9;

    PROCEDURE GETCH;                    {GETS NEXT SOURCE PROGRAM CHARACTER}
    BEGIN IF LINEPTR = LINELENGTH THEN   {AT END OF CURRENT SOURCE LINE}
        BEGIN IF EOF(SOURCEFILE) THEN PRINTABORT(27);

                {READ, PRINT AND INITIALISE NEXT SOURCE LINE}
                WRITE(' '); WRITE(OUTPUTFILE,' ');
                READLN(SOURCEFILE,SOURCELINE); PRINTLN(SOURCELINE);
                LINELENGTH:=LENGTH(SOURCELINE); LINEPTR:=0;

                {COMPENSATE FOR ONE CHARACTER LOOKAHEAD AT END OF LINE}
                SOURCELINE:=CONCAT(SOURCELINE,' '); LINELENGTH:=LINELENGTH+1
        END;

            {GET NEXT CHARACTER FROM CURRENT SOURCE LINE}
            LINEPTR:=LINEPTR+1; CH:=SOURCELINE[LINEPTR]
    END {GETCH};

BEGIN {GETSYM}
        WHILE CH = ' ' DO GETCH;            {IGNORE ANY SPACES BEFORE NEXT SYMBOL}

        WHILE CH = '{' DO                   {IGNORE ANY COMMENTARY SIMILARLY}
        BEGIN REPEAT GETCH UNTIL CH = '}'; REPEAT GETCH UNTIL CH <> ' '
        END;

        IF CH IN ['A'..'Z'] THEN
        BEGIN {IDENTIFIER OR RESERVED WORD}
                ID:='          '; SIZE:=0;
                REPEAT {COLLECT IDENTIFIER CHARACTERS IN ID}
                BEGIN IF SIZE < IDENTMAXSIZE THEN
                        BEGIN SIZE:=SIZE+1; ID[SIZE]:=CH
                        END;
                        GETCH
                END
                UNTIL NOT (CH IN ['A'..'Z','0'..'9']);

                {BINARY SEARCH RESERVED WORD LIST FOR ID}
                LOWER:=1; UPPER:=NOOFRESWRDS;
                REPEAT
                BEGIN MIDDLE:=(LOWER+UPPER) DIV 2;
                        IF ID <= RESWRDS[MIDDLE] THEN UPPER:= MIDDLE-1;
                        IF ID >= RESWRDS[MIDDLE] THEN LOWER:= MIDDLE+1
                END
                UNTIL LOWER > UPPER;

                {SYMBOL IS IDENTIFIER OR APPROPRIATE RESERVED WORD SYMBOL}
                IF ID = RESWRDS[MIDDLE] THEN SYM:=RESWRDSYMS[MIDDLE]
                ELSE SYM:=IDENT
        END
```

```
    ELSE
    IF CH IN ['Ø'..'9'] THEN
    BEGIN {NUMBER}
        SYM:=NUMBR;
        NUM:=Ø; SIZE:=Ø;
        REPEAT {ACCUMULATE VALUE OF NUMBER IN NUM}
        BEGIN SIZE:=SIZE+1; DIGIT:=ORD(CH)-ORD('Ø');
            IF SIZE = NUMBRMAXSIZE THEN {CHECK FOR OVERFLOW}
            IF NUM > (MAXIMUMNUMBR-DIGIT) DIV 1Ø THEN PRINTERROR(25);
            IF SIZE <= NUMBRMAXSIZE THEN NUM:=1Ø*NUM+DIGIT;
            GETCH
        END
        UNTIL NOT (CH IN ['Ø'..'9']);
        IF SIZE > NUMBRMAXSIZE THEN PRINTERROR(25)
    END
    ELSE
    IF CH = ':' THEN
    BEGIN {POSSIBLY ':='}
        GETCH;
        IF CH = '=' THEN
        BEGIN SYM:=BECOMES; GETCH
        END
        ELSE SYM:=NUL
    END
    ELSE
    IF CH = '<' THEN
    BEGIN {'<', '<=' OR '<>'}
        GETCH;
        IF CH = '=' THEN
        BEGIN SYM:=LEQ; GETCH
        END
        ELSE
        IF CH = '>' THEN
        BEGIN SYM:=NEQ; GETCH
        END
        ELSE SYM:=LSS
    END
    ELSE
    IF CH = '>' THEN
    BEGIN {'>' OR '>='}
        GETCH;
        IF CH = '=' THEN
        BEGIN SYM:=GEQ; GETCH
        END
        ELSE SYM:=GTR
    END
    ELSE {FOR ALL OTHER CHARACTERS,
         E.G. '+', '-', '*', '/', '(', ')', '=', ',', ';', '.'}
    BEGIN SYM:=CHARSYMS[CH]; GETCH
    END
END {GETSYM};
```

{!!!! SYNTAX ANALYSIS (PARSING) ROUTINES !!!!}

```
PROCEDURE BLOCK;

    PROCEDURE ENTERID(ID: IDSTRING; IK: IDKIND); {ENTER ID IN IDENTIFIER TABLE}
    BEGIN IF IDCOUNT = IDTABMAXSIZE THEN PRINTABORT(26);
          IDCOUNT:=IDCOUNT+1;
          WITH IDTABLE[IDCOUNT] DO
          BEGIN NAME:=ID; KIND:=IK
          END
    END {ENTERID};

    FUNCTION LOOKUPID(ID: IDSTRING): IDENTNUMBER; {LOOK UP ENTRY NUMBER OF
                                                    ID IN IDENTIFIER TABLE;
                                                    RETURN 0 IF NOT PRESENT}
    VAR   IEN: IDENTNUMBER;

    BEGIN IDTABLE[0].NAME:=ID;
          IEN:=IDCOUNT;
          WHILE IDTABLE[IEN].NAME <> ID DO IEN:=IEN-1; {BACKWARDS TABLE SEARCH}
          LOOKUPID:=IEN
    END {LOOKUPID};

    PROCEDURE CONSTDECLARATION;
    BEGIN (* <CONSTDECLARATION> ::= IDENT = NUMBR *)
          IF SYM = IDENT THEN
          BEGIN GETSYM;
                IF SYM = EQL THEN
                BEGIN GETSYM;
                      IF SYM = NUMBR THEN
                      BEGIN ENTERID(ID,CONSTANT);
                            GETSYM
                      END
                      ELSE PRINTERROR(2)
                END
                ELSE PRINTERROR(3)
          END
          ELSE PRINTERROR(4)
    END {CONSTDECLARATION};

    PROCEDURE VARDECLARATION;
    BEGIN (* <VARDECLARATION> ::= IDENT *)
          IF SYM = IDENT THEN
          BEGIN ENTERID(ID,VARIABLE);
                GETSYM
          END
          ELSE PRINTERROR(4)
    END {VARDECLARATION};
```

```
PROCEDURE STATEMENT;

VAR    INDEX: IDENTNUMBER;

   PROCEDURE EXPRESSION;

      PROCEDURE TERM;

         PROCEDURE FACTOR;
         BEGIN (* <FACTOR> ::= IDENT | NUMBR | ( <EXPRESSION> ) *)
               IF SYM = IDENT THEN
               BEGIN IF LOOKUPID(ID) = Ø THEN PRINTERROR(11);
                        GETSYM
               END
               ELSE
               IF SYM = NUMBR THEN
               BEGIN GETSYM
               END
               ELSE
               IF SYM = LPAREN THEN
               BEGIN GETSYM; EXPRESSION;
                        IF SYM = RPAREN THEN GETSYM ELSE PRINTERROR(22)
               END
               ELSE PRINTERROR(23)
         END {FACTOR};

      BEGIN (* <TERM> ::= <FACTOR> {(*|/) <FACTOR>} *)
            FACTOR;
            WHILE SYM IN [TIMES,SLASH] DO
            BEGIN GETSYM; FACTOR
            END
      END {TERM};

   BEGIN (* <EXPRESSION> ::= [(+|-)] <TERM> {(+|-) <TERM>} *)
         IF SYM IN [PLUS,MINUS] THEN GETSYM;
         TERM;
         WHILE SYM IN [PLUS,MINUS] DO
         BEGIN GETSYM; TERM
         END
   END {EXPRESSION};

   PROCEDURE CONDITION;
   BEGIN (* <CONDITION> ::= <EXPRESSION> (=|<>|<|<=|>|>=) <EXPRESSION> *)
         EXPRESSION;
         IF SYM IN [EQL,NEQ,LSS,LEQ,GTR,GEQ] THEN GETSYM
         ELSE PRINTERROR(2Ø);
         EXPRESSION
   END {CONDITION};
```

```
    BEGIN {STATEMENT}
        IF SYM = IDENT THEN
        BEGIN (* <STATEMENT> ::= IDENT := <EXPRESSION> *)
            INDEX:=LOOKUPID(ID);
            IF INDEX = 0 THEN PRINTERROR(11)
            ELSE
            IF IDTABLE[INDEX].KIND <> VARIABLE THEN PRINTERROR(12);
            GETSYM;
            IF SYM = BECOMES THEN GETSYM ELSE PRINTERROR(13);
            EXPRESSION
        END
        ELSE
        IF SYM = IFSYM THEN
        BEGIN (* <STATEMENT> ::= IF <CONDITION> THEN <STATEMENT> *)
            GETSYM; CONDITION;
            IF SYM = THENSYM THEN GETSYM ELSE PRINTERROR(16);
            STATEMENT
        END
        ELSE
        IF SYM = BEGINSYM THEN
        BEGIN (* <STATEMENT> ::= BEGIN <STATEMENT> {; <STATEMENT>} END *)
            GETSYM; STATEMENT;
            WHILE SYM = SEMICOLON DO
            BEGIN GETSYM; STATEMENT
            END;
            IF SYM = ENDSYM THEN GETSYM ELSE PRINTERROR(17)
        END
        ELSE
        IF SYM = WHILESYM THEN
        BEGIN (* <STATEMENT> ::= WHILE <CONDITION> DO <STATEMENT> *)
            GETSYM; CONDITION;
            IF SYM = DOSYM THEN GETSYM ELSE PRINTERROR(18);
            STATEMENT
        END
        ELSE PRINTERROR(7)
    END {STATEMENT};

BEGIN (* <BLOCK> ::= [CONST <CONSTDECLARATION> {, <CONSTDECLARATION>} ;]
                    VAR <VARDECLARATION> {, <VARDECLARATION>} ;
                    <STATEMENT>                                      *)
    IF SYM = CONSTSYM THEN
    BEGIN GETSYM; CONSTDECLARATION;
        WHILE SYM = COMMA DO
        BEGIN GETSYM; CONSTDECLARATION
        END;
        IF SYM = SEMICOLON THEN GETSYM ELSE PRINTERROR(5)
    END;
    IF SYM = VARSYM THEN
    BEGIN GETSYM; VARDECLARATION;
        WHILE SYM = COMMA DO
        BEGIN GETSYM; VARDECLARATION
        END;
        IF SYM = SEMICOLON THEN GETSYM ELSE PRINTERROR(5)
    END
    ELSE PRINTERROR(1);
    STATEMENT
END {BLOCK};
```

```
{ ¦¦¦¦ MAIN PROGRAM ¦¦¦¦ }

BEGIN {PARSER0 - PL/T: SYNTAX CHECKING WITHOUT ERROR RECOVERY}
      INITIALISE;

      WRITELN; WRITELN;
      WRITELN('PL/T: SYNTAX CHECKING WITHOUT ERROR RECOVERY.');
      WRITELN('*********************************************');
      WRITELN; WRITELN;

      WRITE('PLEASE TYPE IN NAME OF PL/T SOURCE CODE TEXT FILE: ');
      READLN(SOURCENAME);
      ASSIGN(SOURCEFILE,CONCAT(SOURCENAME,'.PLT')); RESET(SOURCEFILE);
      WRITELN;

      WRITE('PLEASE TYPE IN NAME OF OUTPUT LIST FILE ("RETURN" FOR NONE): ');
      READLN(OUTPUTNAME);
      IF OUTPUTNAME = '' THEN OUTPUTNAME:=NULLFILENAME;
      ASSIGN(OUTPUTFILE,CONCAT(OUTPUTNAME,'.LST')); REWRITE(OUTPUTFILE);
      WRITELN;

      WRITELN(OUTPUTFILE); WRITELN(OUTPUTFILE);
      WRITELN(OUTPUTFILE,'PL/T: SYNTAX CHECKING WITHOUT ERROR RECOVERY.');
      WRITELN(OUTPUTFILE,'*********************************************');
      WRITELN(OUTPUTFILE); WRITELN(OUTPUTFILE);

      WRITELN(OUTPUTFILE,'PL/T SOURCE FILE WAS ',CONCAT(SOURCENAME,'.PLT'));
      WRITELN(OUTPUTFILE);

      PRINTNL; PRINTNL;
      PRINTLN('^^^^^^^^^^^^^^^^^^^^^^^^^^^^^^^^^^^^');
      PRINTLN('^ SYNTAX CHECKING STARTS NOW: ^');
      PRINTLN('^^^^^^^^^^^^^^^^^^^^^^^^^^^^^^^^^^^^');
      PRINTNL; PRINTNL;

      {GET NEXT (I.E. FIRST) SOURCE SYMBOL}
      GETSYM;

      (* <PROGRAM> ::= <BLOCK> . *)
      BLOCK;     {ATTEMPT TO PARSE A BLOCK}
      IF SYM <> PERIOD THEN PRINTERROR(9);

      CLOSE(SOURCEFILE);

      PRINTNL; PRINTNL;
      PRINTLN('^^^^^^^^^^^^^^^^^^^^^^^^^^^^^^^^^^^^^^^^^^^^^^^^^^^^');
      PRINTLN('^ SYNTAX CHECKING COMPLETED WITHOUT ERRORS. ^');
      PRINTLN('^^^^^^^^^^^^^^^^^^^^^^^^^^^^^^^^^^^^^^^^^^^^^^^^^^^^');
      PRINTNL; PRINTNL;

      CLOSE(OUTPUTFILE);
      IF OUTPUTNAME = NULLFILENAME THEN ERASE(OUTPUTFILE)
      ELSE WRITELN('(SEE ',CONCAT(OUTPUTNAME,'.LST'),' FOR OUTPUT.)');
      WRITELN
END {PARSER0 - PL/T: SYNTAX CHECKING WITHOUT ERROR RECOVERY}.
```

Chapter 12

COMPILXEC
System Program Listing

```
(*$A-*)
PROGRAM COMPILXEC;            {PL/T: COMPILATION AND MACHINE CODE EXECUTION}

{!!!! DATA DEFINITIONS !!!!}

CONST IDENTMAXSIZE = 8;       {MAX. SIGNIFICANT LENGTH OF IDENTIFIERS}
      NUMBRMAXSIZE = 5;       {MAX. NO. OF DIGITS IN NUMBERS}
      MAXIMUMNUMBR = 32767;   {MAX. NUMERICAL VALUE}
      MAXCHARCODE  = 255;     {MAX. CHARACTER CODE VALUE}
      MAXLINESIZE  = 255;     {MAX. SOURCE LINE LENGTH}
      NOOFRESWRDS  = 8;       {NO. OF PL/T RESERVED WORDS}
      RESWRDLIMIT  = 9;       {MAX. BOUND ON RESERVED WORD SEARCH}
      IDTABMAXSIZE = 50;      {MAX. SIZE OF IDENTIFIER TABLE}
      NOOFERRMESGS = 28;      {NO. OF ERROR MESSAGES}
      NULLFILENAME = '!PLTNULL'; {NAME OF NULL OUTPUT FILE}

      MEMORYSIZE   = 1024;    {NO. OF PL/T MACHINE MEMORY LOCATIONS}
      MAXFUNNUMBER = 6;       {MAX. FUNCTION CODE NUMBER}
      MAXOPRNUMBER = 10;      {MAX. OPR SUB-FUNCTION CODE NUMBER}
      MAXADDRESS   = 1023;    {MAX. MEMORY ADDRESS}
      MAXLITERAL   = 4095;    {MAX. LITERAL OPERAND VALUE}
      MAXARGUMENT  = 4095;    {MAX. INSTRUCTION ARGUMENT VALUE}

TYPE  IDSTRING = STRING[IDENTMAXSIZE];      {IDENTIFIER CHARACTER STRING}
      IDKIND   = (CONSTANT,VARIABLE);       {POSSIBLE KINDS OF IDENTIFIER}
      NUMBRVALUE = 0..MAXIMUMNUMBR;         {UNSIGNED NUMERICAL VALUE}
      RESWRDNUMBER = 1..NOOFRESWRDS;        {RESERVED WORD NUMBER}
      IDENTNUMBER  = 0..IDTABMAXSIZE;       {IDENTIFIER TABLE ENTRY NUMBER}
      ERRORNUMBER  = 1..NOOFERRMESGS;       {ERROR/ERROR MESSAGE NUMBER}
      MESSAGETEXT  = STRING[80];            {ERROR/OTHER MESSAGE TEXT}

      FUNNUMBER  = 0..MAXFUNNUMBER;         {FUNCTION CODE NUMBER}
      OPRNUMBER  = 0..MAXOPRNUMBER;         {OPR SUB-FUNCTION CODE NUMBER}
      ADDRESS    = 0..MAXADDRESS;           {MEMORY ADDRESS}
      LITERAL    = 0..MAXLITERAL;           {LITERAL OPERAND}
      ARGUMENT   = 0..MAXARGUMENT;          {INSTRUCTION ARGUMENT}

      {POSSIBLE KINDS OF SYMBOL, I.E. LEXICAL TOKENS}
      SYMBOL   = (NUL, IDENT, NUMBR, PLUS, MINUS, TIMES, SLASH,
                  EQL, NEQ, LSS, LEQ, GTR, GEQ, BECOMES,
                  LPAREN, RPAREN, COMMA, SEMICOLON, PERIOD,
                  CONSTSYM, VARSYM, BEGINSYM, ENDSYM,
                  IFSYM, THENSYM, WHILESYM, DOSYM);

      {FUNCTION/SUB-FUNCTION REPERTOIRE OF PL/T MACHINE}
      FUNKTION = (LIT,       {0: LOAD LITERAL VALUE ONTO TOP OF STACK}
                  LOD,       {1: LOAD VARIABLE VALUE ONTO TOP OF STACK}
                  STO,       {2: STORE VARIABLE VALUE FROM TOP OF STACK}
                  OPR,       {3: OPERATE ON TOP OF STACK VALUE(S)}
                  JMP,       {4: TRANSFER CONTROL UNCONDITIONALLY}
                  JPF,       {5: TRANSFER CONTROL CONDITIONALLY (IF FALSE)}
                  HLT);      {6: TERMINATE EXECUTION (HALT)}
      {OPR SUB-FUNCTIONS: NEGATE, ADD, SUBTRACT, MULTIPLY, DIVIDE, COMPARE}
      OPRATION = (NEG, ADD, SUB, MPY, DVD,   {CODES 0 TO 10 RESPECTIVELY}
                  CMPEQL, CMPNEQ, CMPLSS,
                  CMPLEQ, CMPGTR, CMPGEQ);

      WORD     = INTEGER;    {PL/T MACHINE WORD (16 BITS)}
```

```
VAR   SOURCEFILE, OUTPUTFILE: TEXT;          {SOURCE AND OUTPUT FILES}
      SOURCENAME, OUTPUTNAME: STRING[20];    {SOURCE AND OUTPUT FILE NAMES}

      SOURCELINE: STRING[MAXLINESIZE];       {CURRENT SOURCE LINE}
      LINELENGTH: 0..MAXLINESIZE;            {LENGTH OF CURRENT SOURCE LINE}
      LINEPTR: 0..MAXLINESIZE;               {CURRENT POSITION WITHIN SOURCE LINE}

      CH: CHAR;            {MOST RECENTLY RECOGNISED CHARACTER}
      SYM: SYMBOL;         {MOST RECENTLY RECOGNISED SYMBOL}
      ID: IDSTRING;        {MOST RECENTLY RECOGNISED IDENTIFIER}
      NUM: NUMBRVALUE;     {MOST RECENTLY RECOGNISED NUMBER}

      CHARSYMS: ARRAY[CHAR] OF SYMBOL;       {SYMBOLS FOR INDIVIDUAL CHARACTERS}

      RESWRDS: ARRAY[RESWRDNUMBER] OF IDSTRING;      {RESERVED WORD LIST}
      RESWRDSYMS: ARRAY[RESWRDNUMBER] OF SYMBOL;     {SYMBOLS FOR RESERVED WORDS}

      IDTABLE: ARRAY[IDENTNUMBER] OF         {IDENTIFIER TABLE}
            RECORD NAME: IDSTRING;           {IDENTIFIER NAME}
                   KIND: IDKIND;             {IDENTIFIER KIND}
                   CASE IDKIND OF            {IDENTIFIER VALUE VARIANT}
            CONSTANT: (LITERALVALUE: LITERAL);       {LITERAL VALUE}
            VARIABLE: (ADDRESSVALUE: ADDRESS)        {ADDRESS VALUE}
                END;
      IDCOUNT: IDENTNUMBER;                  {IDENTIFIER TABLE ENTRY COUNT}

      ERRMESGS: ARRAY[ERRORNUMBER] OF MESSAGETEXT; {ERROR MESSAGE LIST}

      FUNMNEMONICS: ARRAY[FUNNUMBER] OF STRING[3]; {FUNCTION MNEMONIC LIST}
      OPRMNEMONICS: ARRAY[OPRNUMBER] OF STRING[6]; {OPRATION MNEMONIC LIST}

      HEXDIGITS: STRING[16];     {HEXADECIMAL DIGIT ALPHABET}

      PERLINEMCODE: BOOLEAN;     {PER LINE M/C CODE LISTING? (USER OPTION)}
      TRACEWANTED: BOOLEAN;      {M/C CODE EXECUTION TRACE? (USER OPTION)}
      ANSWERCH: CHAR;            {FOR RECEIPT OF USER ANSWERS TO QUESTIONS}

      MEMORY: ARRAY[ADDRESS] OF WORD;     {MAIN STORE OF PL/T MACHINE}

      NEXTIADDRESS: 0..MEMORYSIZE;  {ADDRESS OF NEXT FREE INSTRUCTION LOCATION}
      NEXTVADDRESS: 0..MEMORYSIZE;  {ADDRESS OF NEXT FREE VARS STACK LOCATION}

      PROGLOWERB, PROGUPPERB: ADDRESS;    {M/C CODE PROGRAM ADDRESS BOUNDS}
      VARSLOWERB, VARSUPPERB: ADDRESS;    {VARIABLES STACK ADDRESS BOUNDS}
      VARSTACKBASE: ADDRESS;              {VARIABLES STACK BASE ADDRESS}
      TRACLOWERB, TRACUPPERB: INTEGER;    {EXECUTION TRACE ADDRESS BOUNDS}

      INSTRUCTION: WORD;     {INSTRUCTION ASSEMBLY/DISASSEMBLY BUFFER...}
      FUNCODE: FUNNUMBER;    {FUNCTION CODE PART OF INSTRUCTION}
      ARGCODE: ARGUMENT;     {ARGUMENT CODE PART OF INSTRUCTION}
      HEXINSTR: STRING[4];   {INSTRUCTION IN HEXADECIMAL FORM}
```

{ ¦¦¦¦ INITIALISATION AND PRINTOUT ROUTINES ¦¦¦¦}

PROCEDURE INITIALISE;   {INITIALISES GLOBAL VARIABLES}

  PROCEDURE INITSYMBOLS;   {INITIALISES CHARSYMS AND RESWRDS/SYMS}

  VAR   ICH: CHAR;

  BEGIN {INITIALISE SYMBOLS FOR INDIVIDUAL CHARACTERS}
     FOR ICH:=CHR(Ø) TO CHR(MAXCHARCODE) DO CHARSYMS[ICH]:=NUL;
     CHARSYMS['+']:=PLUS;   CHARSYMS['-']:=MINUS;   CHARSYMS['*']:=TIMES;
     CHARSYMS['/']:=SLASH; CHARSYMS['(']:=LPAREN;   CHARSYMS[')']:=RPAREN;
     CHARSYMS['=']:=EQL;   CHARSYMS['<']:=LSS;   CHARSYMS['>']:=GTR;
     CHARSYMS[',']:=COMMA; CHARSYMS[';']:=SEMICOLON; CHARSYMS['.']:=PERIOD;

     {INITIALISE RESERVED WORD AND ASSOCIATED SYMBOL LISTS, ALPHABETICALLY}
     RESWRDS[1]:='BEGIN   ';   RESWRDSYMS[1]:=BEGINSYM;
     RESWRDS[2]:='CONST   ';   RESWRDSYMS[2]:=CONSTSYM;
     RESWRDS[3]:='DO   ';   RESWRDSYMS[3]:=DOSYM;
     RESWRDS[4]:='END   ';   RESWRDSYMS[4]:=ENDSYM;
     RESWRDS[5]:='IF   ';   RESWRDSYMS[5]:=IFSYM;
     RESWRDS[6]:='THEN   ';   RESWRDSYMS[6]:=THENSYM;
     RESWRDS[7]:='VAR   ';   RESWRDSYMS[7]:=VARSYM;
     RESWRDS[8]:='WHILE   ';   RESWRDSYMS[8]:=WHILESYM
  END {INITSYMBOLS};

  PROCEDURE INITERRMESGS;   {INITIALISES ERROR MESSAGE LIST}
  BEGIN ERRMESGS[1] :='"VAR" DECLARATION(S) EXPECTED.';
     ERRMESGS[2] :='"=" MUST BE FOLLOWED BY A NUMBER.';
     ERRMESGS[3] :='IDENTIFIER MUST BE FOLLOWED BY "=".';
     ERRMESGS[4] :='"CONST" OR "VAR" MUST BE FOLLOWED BY AN IDENTIFIER.';
     ERRMESGS[5] :='SEMICOLON OR COMMA MISSING.';
     ERRMESGS[6] :='SYSTEM FAULT - PLEASE REPORT TO TUTOR.';
     ERRMESGS[7] :='STATEMENT EXPECTED.';
     ERRMESGS[8] :=ERRMESGS[6];
     ERRMESGS[9] :='FULL STOP EXPECTED.';
     ERRMESGS[10]:=ERRMESGS[6];
     ERRMESGS[11]:='UNDECLARED IDENTIFIER.';
     ERRMESGS[12]:='ASSIGNMENT TO CONSTANT IS NOT ALLOWED.';
     ERRMESGS[13]:='ASSIGNMENT OPERATOR ":=" EXPECTED.';
     ERRMESGS[14]:=ERRMESGS[6];
     ERRMESGS[15]:=ERRMESGS[6];
     ERRMESGS[16]:='"THEN" EXPECTED.';
     ERRMESGS[17]:='SEMICOLON OR "END" EXPECTED.';
     ERRMESGS[18]:='"DO" EXPECTED.';
     ERRMESGS[19]:=ERRMESGS[6];
     ERRMESGS[20]:='RELATIONAL OPERATOR EXPECTED.';
     ERRMESGS[21]:=ERRMESGS[6];
     ERRMESGS[22]:='RIGHT PARENTHESIS MISSING.';
     ERRMESGS[23]:='IDENTIFIER, NUMBER OR "(" EXPECTED.';
     ERRMESGS[24]:=ERRMESGS[6];
     ERRMESGS[25]:='NUMBER TOO LARGE.';
     ERRMESGS[26]:='IDENTIFIER TABLE OVERFLOW.';
     ERRMESGS[27]:='SOURCE PROGRAM INCOMPLETE.';
     ERRMESGS[28]:='MACHINE CODE PROGRAM TOO BIG.'
  END {INITERRMESGS};

```
    PROCEDURE INITMNEMONICS;                {INITIALISES FUNCTION MNEMONIC LISTS}
    BEGIN FUNMNEMONICS[0]:='LIT';           FUNMNEMONICS[1]:='LOD';
          FUNMNEMONICS[2]:='STO';           FUNMNEMONICS[3]:='OPR';
          FUNMNEMONICS[4]:='JMP';           FUNMNEMONICS[5]:='JPF';
          FUNMNEMONICS[6]:='HLT';
          OPRMNEMONICS[0]:='NEG';
          OPRMNEMONICS[1]:='ADD';           OPRMNEMONICS[2]:='SUB';
          OPRMNEMONICS[3]:='MPY';           OPRMNEMONICS[4]:='DVD';
          OPRMNEMONICS[5]:='CMPEQL';        OPRMNEMONICS[6]:='CMPNEQ';
          OPRMNEMONICS[7]:='CMPLSS';        OPRMNEMONICS[8]:='CMPLEQ';
          OPRMNEMONICS[9]:='CMPGTR';        OPRMNEMONICS[10]:='CMPGEQ'
    END {INITMNEMONICS};


BEGIN {INITIALISE SYMBOLS, IDENTIFIER TABLE, ERROR MESSAGES AND MNEMONIC LISTS}
      INITSYMBOLS;        IDCOUNT:=0;        INITERRMESGS;       INITMNEMONICS;

      {INITIALISE LEXICAL STATE VARIABLES AND HEXADECIMAL DIGIT ALPHABET}
      LINELENGTH:=0; LINEPTR:=0; CH:=' ';       HEXDIGITS:='0123456789ABCDEF';

      {INITIALISE STORAGE ALLOCATION ADDRESSES}
      NEXTIADDRESS:=0; NEXTVADDRESS:=0
END {INITIALISE};


(*$I PRINTS.PAS*) {PRINTLN, PRINTNL, PRINTERROR, PRINTABORT; ~AS IN PARSER0}

PROCEDURE HEXSTRING(INSTRUCTION: WORD); FORWARD;

PROCEDURE PRINTMCODE(THISADDRESS: ADDRESS); {WRITES M/C INSTRUCTION LINE
                                             (DECODED) TO SCREEN AND FILE}
BEGIN INSTRUCTION:=MEMORY[THISADDRESS]; HEXSTRING(INSTRUCTION);
      FUNCODE:=INSTRUCTION DIV 4096; ARGCODE:=INSTRUCTION MOD 4096;

      WRITE('->@',THISADDRESS:3,':',' (#',HEXINSTR,'#) ');
      WRITE(' ':4,FUNMNEMONICS[FUNCODE],' ':4);
      WRITE(OUTPUTFILE,'->@',THISADDRESS:3,':',' (#',HEXINSTR,'#) ');
      WRITE(OUTPUTFILE,' ':4,FUNMNEMONICS[FUNCODE],' ':4);

      CASE FUNCODE OF
  0: BEGIN WRITE(' ',ARGCODE:1); WRITE(OUTPUTFILE,' ',ARGCODE:1)
{LIT} END;
  1: BEGIN WRITE('@S[',ARGCODE:1,']'); WRITE(OUTPUTFILE,'@S[',ARGCODE:1,']')
{LOD} END;
  2: BEGIN WRITE('@S[',ARGCODE:1,']'); WRITE(OUTPUTFILE,'@S[',ARGCODE:1,']')
{STO} END;
  3: BEGIN WRITE(' ',ARGCODE:1,'{':4,OPRMNEMONICS[ARGCODE],'}');
{OPR}      WRITE(OUTPUTFILE,' ',ARGCODE:1,'{':4,OPRMNEMONICS[ARGCODE],'}')
           END;
  4: BEGIN WRITE('@',ARGCODE:1); WRITE(OUTPUTFILE,'@',ARGCODE:1)
{JMP} END;
  5: BEGIN WRITE('@',ARGCODE:1); WRITE(OUTPUTFILE,'@',ARGCODE:1)
{JPF} END;
  6: BEGIN WRITE(' ',ARGCODE:1); WRITE(OUTPUTFILE,' ',ARGCODE:1)
{HLT} END
      END {CASE};

      WRITELN; WRITELN(OUTPUTFILE)
END {PRINTMCODE};
```

```
PROCEDURE PRINTIDENT(THISIDENT: IDENTNUMBER); {WRITES IDENTIFIER VALUE LINE
                                                   (DECODED) TO SCREEN AND FILE}
BEGIN WITH IDTABLE[THISIDENT] DO
      BEGIN WRITE('-> ',' ':5,NAME,'=');
            WRITE(OUTPUTFILE,'-> ',' ':5,NAME,'=');
            CASE KIND OF
  CONSTANT: BEGIN WRITELN(' ',LITERALVALUE:1);
                  WRITELN(OUTPUTFILE,' ',LITERALVALUE:1)
            END;
  VARIABLE: BEGIN WRITELN('@S[',ADDRESSVALUE:1,']');
                  WRITELN(OUTPUTFILE,'@S[',ADDRESSVALUE:1,']')
            END
            END {CASE}
      END
END {PRINTIDENT};

PROCEDURE PRINTPROGMCODE;               {PRINTS PROGRAM M/C CODE SUMMARY}


VAR   THISADDRESS: ADDRESS; THISIDENT: IDENTNUMBER;

BEGIN PRINTNL; PRINTNL;
      PRINTLN('IDENTIFIERS SUMMARY:-');
      PRINTLN('==================');
      FOR THISIDENT:=1 TO IDCOUNT DO PRINTIDENT(THISIDENT);
      PRINTNL;
      PRINTLN('MACHINE CODE SUMMARY:-');
      PRINTLN('==================');
      FOR THISADDRESS:=0 TO NEXTIADDRESS-1 DO PRINTMCODE(THISADDRESS);
      PRINTNL; PRINTNL
END {PRINTPROGMCODE};

PROCEDURE PRINTVARIABLE(THISADDRESS: ADDRESS); {WRITES VARIABLE'S VALUE LINE
                                                   (DECODED) TO SCREEN AND FILE}
BEGIN WITH IDTABLE[IDCOUNT-VARSUPPERB+THISADDRESS] DO
      BEGIN WRITE('@S[',THISADDRESS:1,']',' ':3,NAME,':=');
            WRITELN(MEMORY[VARSTACKBASE+THISADDRESS]:1);
            WRITE(OUTPUTFILE,'@S[',THISADDRESS:1,']',' ':3,NAME,':=');
            WRITELN(OUTPUTFILE,MEMORY[VARSTACKBASE+THISADDRESS]:1)
      END
END {PRINTVARIABLE};

PROCEDURE PRINTRESULTS;                 {PRINTS PROGRAM RESULTS SUMMARY}


VAR   THISADDRESS: ADDRESS;

BEGIN PRINTNL; PRINTNL;
      PRINTLN('VAR RESULTS SUMMARY:-');
      PRINTLN('==================');
      FOR THISADDRESS:=VARSLOWERB TO VARSUPPERB DO PRINTVARIABLE(THISADDRESS);
      PRINTNL; PRINTNL
END {PRINTRESULTS};
```

```
(*$I GETSYM.PAS*) {GETSYM, GETCH; ~AS IN PARSER0}

{!!!! CODE GENERATION AND CONVERSION ROUTINES !!!!}

PROCEDURE GENERATE(FUNCODE: FUNNUMBER; ARGCODE: ARGUMENT); {GENERATES MACHINE
                                                            CODE INSTRUCTIONS}
BEGIN IF NEXTIADDRESS > MAXADDRESS THEN PRINTABORT(28);
      INSTRUCTION:=FUNCODE*4096+ARGCODE;
      MEMORY[NEXTIADDRESS]:=INSTRUCTION;
      IF PERLINEMCODE THEN PRINTMCODE(NEXTIADDRESS);
      NEXTIADDRESS:=NEXTIADDRESS+1
END {GENERATE};

PROCEDURE BACKFILL(FILLADDRESS: ADDRESS); {PATCHES UP JUMP INSTRUCTIONS WITH
                                           MISSING FORWARD ADDRESS ARGUMENTS}
BEGIN IF NEXTIADDRESS > MAXADDRESS THEN PRINTABORT(28);
      MEMORY[FILLADDRESS]:=MEMORY[FILLADDRESS]+NEXTIADDRESS;
      IF PERLINEMCODE THEN PRINTMCODE(FILLADDRESS)
END {BACKFILL};

PROCEDURE HEXSTRING{(INSTRUCTION: WORD)}; {CONVERTS BINARY INSTRUCTION TO HEX}

VAR   DIGITNO: 1..4;

BEGIN HEXINSTR:='0000';
      FOR DIGITNO:=4 DOWNTO 1 DO
      BEGIN HEXINSTR[DIGITNO]:=HEXDIGITS[(INSTRUCTION MOD 16)+1];
            INSTRUCTION:=INSTRUCTION DIV 16
      END
END {HEXSTRING};
```

```
{!!!! SYNTAX ANALYSIS WITH CODE SYNTHESIS ROUTINES !!!!}

PROCEDURE BLOCK;

   PROCEDURE ENTERID(ID: IDSTRING; IK: IDKIND); {ENTER ID IN IDENTIFIER TABLE}
   BEGIN IF IDCOUNT = IDTABMAXSIZE THEN PRINTABORT(26);
         IDCOUNT:=IDCOUNT+1;
         WITH IDTABLE[IDCOUNT] DO
         BEGIN NAME:=ID; KIND:=IK;
               CASE KIND OF
      CONSTANT: BEGIN IF NUM > MAXLITERAL THEN PRINTERROR(25);
                      LITERALVALUE:=NUM
                END;
      VARIABLE: BEGIN IF NEXTVADDRESS > MAXADDRESS THEN PRINTABORT(28);
                      ADDRESSVALUE:=NEXTVADDRESS; NEXTVADDRESS:=NEXTVADDRESS+1
                END
                END {CASE}
         END;
         IF PERLINEMCODE THEN PRINTIDENT(IDCOUNT)
   END {ENTERID};

   FUNCTION LOOKUPID(ID: IDSTRING): IDENTNUMBER; {LOOK UP ENTRY NUMBER OF
                                                  ID IN IDENTIFIER TABLE;
                                                  RETURN Ø IF NOT PRESENT}
   VAR   IEN: IDENTNUMBER;

   BEGIN IDTABLE[Ø].NAME:=ID;
         IEN:=IDCOUNT;
         WHILE IDTABLE[IEN].NAME <> ID DO IEN:=IEN-1; {BACKWARDS TABLE SEARCH}
         LOOKUPID:=IEN
   END {LOOKUPID};

   PROCEDURE CONSTDECLARATION;
   BEGIN (* <CONSTDECLARATION> ::= IDENT = NUMBR *)
         IF SYM = IDENT THEN
         BEGIN GETSYM;
               IF SYM = EQL THEN
               BEGIN GETSYM;
                     IF SYM = NUMBR THEN
                     BEGIN ENTERID(ID,CONSTANT);
                           GETSYM
                     END
                     ELSE PRINTERROR(2)
               END
               ELSE PRINTERROR(3)
         END
         ELSE PRINTERROR(4)
   END {CONSTDECLARATION};

   PROCEDURE VARDECLARATION;
   BEGIN (* <VARDECLARATION> ::= IDENT *)
         IF SYM = IDENT THEN
         BEGIN ENTERID(ID,VARIABLE);
               GETSYM
         END
         ELSE PRINTERROR(4)
   END {VARDECLARATION};
```

```
PROCEDURE STATEMENT;

VAR  INDEX: IDENTNUMBER; WHILADDRESS, DOADDRESS, THENADDRESS: Ø..MEMORYSIZE;

   PROCEDURE EXPRESSION; VAR  PLUSORMINUS: SYMBOL;

      PROCEDURE TERM;     VAR  TIMESORSLASH: SYMBOL;

         PROCEDURE FACTOR; VAR INDEX: IDENTNUMBER;
         BEGIN (* <FACTOR> ::= IDENT | NUMBR | ( <EXPRESSION> ) *)
              IF SYM = IDENT THEN
              BEGIN INDEX:=LOOKUPID(ID);
                    IF INDEX = Ø THEN PRINTERROR(11);
                    WITH IDTABLE[INDEX] DO
                    BEGIN CASE KIND OF
                  CONSTANT: GENERATE(ORD(LIT),LITERALVALUE);
                  VARIABLE: GENERATE(ORD(LOD),ADDRESSVALUE)
                          END {CASE}
                    END;
                    GETSYM
              END
              ELSE
              IF SYM = NUMBR THEN
              BEGIN IF NUM > MAXLITERAL THEN PRINTERROR(25);
                    GENERATE(ORD(LIT),NUM); GETSYM
              END
              ELSE
              IF SYM = LPAREN THEN
              BEGIN GETSYM; EXPRESSION;
                    IF SYM = RPAREN THEN GETSYM ELSE PRINTERROR(22)
              END
              ELSE PRINTERROR(23)
         END {FACTOR};

      BEGIN (* <TERM> ::= <FACTOR> {(*|/) <FACTOR>} *)
           FACTOR;
           WHILE SYM IN [TIMES,SLASH] DO
           BEGIN TIMESORSLASH:=SYM; GETSYM; FACTOR;
                 IF TIMESORSLASH = TIMES THEN GENERATE(ORD(OPR),ORD(MPY))
                 ELSE GENERATE(ORD(OPR),ORD(DVD))
           END
      END {TERM};

   BEGIN (* <EXPRESSION> ::= [(+|-)] <TERM> {(+|-) <TERM>} *)
        IF SYM IN [PLUS,MINUS] THEN
        BEGIN PLUSORMINUS:=SYM; GETSYM
        END
        ELSE PLUSORMINUS:=PLUS;
        TERM;
        IF PLUSORMINUS = MINUS THEN GENERATE(ORD(OPR),ORD(NEG));
        WHILE SYM IN [PLUS,MINUS] DO
        BEGIN PLUSORMINUS:=SYM; GETSYM; TERM;
              IF PLUSORMINUS = PLUS THEN GENERATE(ORD(OPR),ORD(ADD))
              ELSE GENERATE(ORD(OPR),ORD(SUB))
        END
   END {EXPRESSION};
```

```
      PROCEDURE CONDITION;  VAR  COMPARATOR: SYMBOL;
      BEGIN (* <CONDITION> ::= <EXPRESSION> (=|<>|<|<=|>|>=) <EXPRESSION> *)
            EXPRESSION;
            IF SYM IN [EQL,NEQ,LSS,LEQ,GTR,GEQ] THEN
            BEGIN COMPARATOR:=SYM; GETSYM
            END
            ELSE PRINTERROR(20);
            EXPRESSION;
            CASE COMPARATOR OF
        EQL:GENERATE(ORD(OPR),ORD(CMPEQL)); NEQ:GENERATE(ORD(OPR),ORD(CMPNEQ));
        LSS:GENERATE(ORD(OPR),ORD(CMPLSS)); LEQ:GENERATE(ORD(OPR),ORD(CMPLEQ));
        GTR:GENERATE(ORD(OPR),ORD(CMPGTR)); GEQ:GENERATE(ORD(OPR),ORD(CMPGEQ))
            END {CASE}
      END {CONDITION};

BEGIN {STATEMENT}
      IF SYM = IDENT THEN
      BEGIN (* <STATEMENT> ::= IDENT := <EXPRESSION> *)
            INDEX:=LOOKUPID(ID);
            IF INDEX = 0 THEN PRINTERROR(11)
            ELSE
            IF IDTABLE[INDEX].KIND <> VARIABLE THEN PRINTERROR(12);
            GETSYM;
            IF SYM = BECOMES THEN GETSYM ELSE PRINTERROR(13);
            EXPRESSION;
            WITH IDTABLE[INDEX] DO GENERATE(ORD(STO),ADDRESSVALUE)
      END
      ELSE
      IF SYM = IFSYM THEN
      BEGIN (* <STATEMENT> ::= IF <CONDITION> THEN <STATEMENT> *)
            GETSYM; CONDITION;
            THENADDRESS:=NEXTIADDRESS; GENERATE(ORD(JPF),0);
            IF SYM = THENSYM THEN GETSYM ELSE PRINTERROR(16);
            STATEMENT;
            BACKFILL(THENADDRESS)
      END
      ELSE
      IF SYM = BEGINSYM THEN
      BEGIN (* <STATEMENT> ::= BEGIN <STATEMENT> {; <STATEMENT>} END *)
            GETSYM; STATEMENT;
            WHILE SYM = SEMICOLON DO
            BEGIN GETSYM; STATEMENT
            END;
            IF SYM = ENDSYM THEN GETSYM ELSE PRINTERROR(17)
      END
      ELSE
      IF SYM = WHILESYM THEN
      BEGIN (* <STATEMENT> ::= WHILE <CONDITION> DO <STATEMENT> *)
            WHILADDRESS:=NEXTIADDRESS;
            GETSYM; CONDITION;
            DOADDRESS:=NEXTIADDRESS; GENERATE(ORD(JPF),0);
            IF SYM = DOSYM THEN GETSYM ELSE PRINTERROR(18);
            STATEMENT;
            GENERATE(ORD(JMP),WHILADDRESS); BACKFILL(DOADDRESS)
      END
      ELSE PRINTERROR(7)
END {STATEMENT};
```

```
BEGIN (* <BLOCK> ::= [CONST <CONSTDECLARATION> {, <CONSTDECLARATION>} ;]
                     VAR <VARDECLARATION> {, <VARDECLARATION>} ;
                     <STATEMENT>                                              *)
      IF SYM = CONSTSYM THEN
      BEGIN GETSYM; CONSTDECLARATION;
            WHILE SYM = COMMA DO
            BEGIN GETSYM; CONSTDECLARATION
            END;
            IF SYM = SEMICOLON THEN GETSYM ELSE PRINTERROR(5)
      END;
      IF SYM = VARSYM THEN
      BEGIN GETSYM; VARDECLARATION;
            WHILE SYM = COMMA DO
            BEGIN GETSYM; VARDECLARATION
            END;
            IF SYM = SEMICOLON THEN GETSYM ELSE PRINTERROR(5)
      END
      ELSE PRINTERROR(1);
      STATEMENT;
      GENERATE(ORD(HLT),0)
END {BLOCK};



{!!!! USER DIALOGUE ROUTINES !!!!}

PROCEDURE OPTIONDIALOGUE;                {DETERMINES COMPILATION OPTION SETTINGS}
BEGIN WRITELN('DO YOU WANT A MACHINE CODE LISTING AFTER EACH SOURCE LINE?');
      WRITE('ANSWER Y(ES) IF YOU DO, OTHERWISE NO WILL BE ASSUMED: ');
      READLN(ANSWERCH); WRITELN;
      IF ANSWERCH = 'Y' THEN PERLINEMCODE:=TRUE ELSE PERLINEMCODE:=FALSE
END {OPTIONDIALOGUE};

PROCEDURE TRACEDIALOGUE;                 {DETERMINES EXECUTION TRACE BOUNDS}
BEGIN WRITELN('DO YOU WANT A TRACE, FULL OR PARTIAL, OF PROGRAM EXECUTION?');
      WRITE('ANSWER F(ULL) OR P(ARTIAL), OTHERWISE NONE WILL BE ASSUMED: ');
      READLN(ANSWERCH); WRITELN;
      IF ANSWERCH = 'F' THEN
      BEGIN TRACEWANTED:=TRUE; TRACLOWERB:=PROGLOWERB; TRACUPPERB:=PROGUPPERB
      END
      ELSE
      IF ANSWERCH = 'P' THEN
      BEGIN TRACEWANTED:=TRUE;
            WRITELN('PLEASE TYPE LOWER AND UPPER BOUNDS OF TRACE, IN ORDER;');
            WRITE('THESE MUST BE BETWEEN ',PROGLOWERB:1,' AND ',PROGUPPERB:1);
            WRITE(': '); READLN(TRACLOWERB,TRACUPPERB); WRITELN;
            IF TRACLOWERB < PROGLOWERB THEN TRACLOWERB:=PROGLOWERB;
            IF TRACUPPERB > PROGUPPERB THEN TRACUPPERB:=PROGUPPERB;
            IF TRACLOWERB > TRACUPPERB THEN TRACEWANTED:=FALSE
      END
      ELSE TRACEWANTED:=FALSE
END {TRACEDIALOGUE};

(*$I INTERP.PAS*) {INTERPRETER; SEE LISTING FOLLOWING MAIN PROGRAM BELOW}
```

```
{!!!! COMPILATION AND EXECUTION CONTROLLING ROUTINES !!!!}

PROCEDURE COMPILE;                        {COMPILES A PL/T PROGRAM}
BEGIN OPTIONDIALOGUE; {GET THE USER TO SPECIFY HIS COMPILATION OPTIONS}

      PRINTNL; PRINTNL;
      PRINTLN('^^^^^^^^^^^^^^^^^^^^^^^^^^^^^');
      PRINTLN('^ COMPILATION STARTS NOW: ^');
      PRINTLN('^^^^^^^^^^^^^^^^^^^^^^^^^^^^^');
      PRINTNL; PRINTNL;

      GETSYM;           {GET NEXT (I.E. FIRST) SOURCE SYMBOL}

      (* <PROGRAM> ::= <BLOCK> . *)
      BLOCK;            {ATTEMPT TO COMPILE A BLOCK}
      IF SYM <> PERIOD THEN PRINTERROR(9);

      PRINTPROGMCODE; {PRINT MACHINE CODE/IDENTIFIER SUMMARY FOR PROGRAM}

      PRINTNL; PRINTNL;
      PRINTLN('^^^^^^^^^^^^^^^^^^^^^^^^^^^^^^^^^^^^^^^^^^^^');
      PRINTLN('^ COMPILATION COMPLETED WITHOUT ERRORS. ^');
      PRINTLN('^^^^^^^^^^^^^^^^^^^^^^^^^^^^^^^^^^^^^^^^^^^^');
      PRINTNL; PRINTNL
END {COMPILE};

PROCEDURE HANDOVER;                  {ARRANGES COMPILER/EXECUTER TRANSITION}
BEGIN PROGLOWERB:=0; PROGUPPERB:=NEXTIADDRESS-1;
      VARSLOWERB:=0; VARSUPPERB:=NEXTVADDRESS-1;
      IF VARSUPPERB > (MAXADDRESS-NEXTIADDRESS) THEN PRINTABORT(28);
      VARSTACKBASE:=NEXTIADDRESS
END {HANDOVER};

PROCEDURE EXECUTE;                        {EXECUTES A PL/T PROGRAM}
BEGIN TRACEDIALOGUE;  {GET THE USER TO SPECIFY HIS EXECUTION TRACE BOUNDS}

      PRINTNL; PRINTNL;
      PRINTLN('^^^^^^^^^^^^^^^^^^^^^^^^^^^^^^^^^^^^^^^^^^');
      PRINTLN('^ MACHINE CODE EXECUTION STARTS NOW: ^');
      PRINTLN('^^^^^^^^^^^^^^^^^^^^^^^^^^^^^^^^^^^^^^^^^^');
      PRINTNL; PRINTNL;

      INTERPRET;        {ATTEMPT TO EXECUTE PROGRAM, INTERPRETIVELY}

      PRINTRESULTS;     {PRINT RESULTS SUMMARY FOR PROGRAM}

      PRINTNL; PRINTNL;
      PRINTLN('^^^^^^^^^^^^^^^^^^^^^^^^^^^^^^^^^^^^^^^^^^');
      PRINTLN('^ MACHINE CODE EXECUTION COMPLETED. ^');
      PRINTLN('^^^^^^^^^^^^^^^^^^^^^^^^^^^^^^^^^^^^^^^^^^');
      PRINTNL; PRINTNL
END {EXECUTE};
```

```
{¦¦¦¦ MAIN PROGRAM ¦¦¦¦}

BEGIN {COMPILER/EXECUTER - PL/T: COMPILATION AND MACHINE CODE EXECUTION}
      INITIALISE;

      WRITELN; WRITELN;
      WRITELN('PL/T: COMPILATION AND MACHINE CODE EXECUTION.');
      WRITELN('*********************************************');
      WRITELN; WRITELN;

      WRITE('PLEASE TYPE IN NAME OF PL/T SOURCE CODE TEXT FILE: ');
      READLN(SOURCENAME);
      ASSIGN(SOURCEFILE,CONCAT(SOURCENAME,'.PLT')); RESET(SOURCEFILE);
      WRITELN;

      WRITE('PLEASE TYPE IN NAME OF OUTPUT LIST FILE ("RETURN" FOR NONE): ');
      READLN(OUTPUTNAME);
      IF OUTPUTNAME = '' THEN OUTPUTNAME:=NULLFILENAME;
      ASSIGN(OUTPUTFILE,CONCAT(OUTPUTNAME,'.LST')); REWRITE(OUTPUTFILE);
      WRITELN;

      WRITELN(OUTPUTFILE); WRITELN(OUTPUTFILE);
      WRITELN(OUTPUTFILE,'PL/T: COMPILATION AND MACHINE CODE EXECUTION.');
      WRITELN(OUTPUTFILE,'*********************************************');
      WRITELN(OUTPUTFILE); WRITELN(OUTPUTFILE);

      WRITELN(OUTPUTFILE,'PL/T SOURCE FILE WAS ',CONCAT(SOURCENAME,'.PLT'));
      WRITELN(OUTPUTFILE);

      COMPILE;        {COMPILE PL/T PROGRAM}

      CLOSE(SOURCEFILE);

      HANDOVER;       {COMPILER/EXECUTER TRANSITION}

      EXECUTE;        {EXECUTE PL/T PROGRAM}

      CLOSE(OUTPUTFILE);
      IF OUTPUTNAME = NULLFILENAME THEN ERASE(OUTPUTFILE)
      ELSE WRITELN('(SEE ',CONCAT(OUTPUTNAME,'.LST'),' FOR OUTPUT.)');
      WRITELN
END {COMPILER/EXECUTER - PL/T: COMPILATION AND MACHINE CODE EXECUTION}.
```

```
{↓↓↓↓ INTERPRETER ROUTINE ↓↓↓↓}

PROCEDURE INTERPRET;              {PL/T: MACHINE CODE PROGRAM INTERPRETATION}

VAR   PP: ADDRESS;               {PROGRAM POINTER REGISTER}
      SB: ADDRESS;               {EXECUTION STACK BASE REGISTER}
      SP: ADDRESS;               {(TOP OF) STACK POINTER REGISTER}
      IR: WORD;                  {CURRENT INSTRUCTION REGISTER}
      FUN: FUNNUMBER;            {FUNCTION CODE PART OF CURRENT INSTRUCTION}
      ARG: ARGUMENT;             {ARGUMENT CODE PART OF CURRENT INSTRUCTION}
      TRACEVALID: BOOLEAN;          {TRACING VALIDITY FLAG}
      CPUSTATE: (RUNNING,HALTED);   {STATE OF PL/T MACHINE}

   PROCEDURE PRINTREGISTERS;   {WRITES REGISTER TRACE TO SCREEN AND FILE}
   BEGIN WRITE('PP=',PP:2,' ':3,'SP=',SP:2,' ':3);
        WRITE('S[',(SP-1):1,']=',MEMORY[SB+SP-1]:1);
        WRITELN(' ':3,'S[',SP:1,']=',MEMORY[SB+SP]:1);
        WRITE(OUTPUTFILE,'PP=',PP:2,' ':3,'SP=',SP:2,' ':3);
        WRITE(OUTPUTFILE,'S[',(SP-1):1,']=',MEMORY[SB+SP-1]:1);
        WRITELN(OUTPUTFILE,' ':3,'S[',SP:1,']=',MEMORY[SB+SP]:1)
   END {PRINTREGISTERS};

BEGIN {INTERPRET - PL/T: MACHINE CODE PROGRAM INTERPRETATION}

      SB:=VARSTACKBASE;            {INITIALISE STACK BASE REGISTER}
      FOR SP:=VARSLOWERB TO VARSUPPERB DO
      MEMORY[SB+SP]:=-32767;    {INITIALISE VARIABLES TO "UNDEFINED"}
      SP:=VARSUPPERB;          {INITIALISE STACK POINTER REGISTER}
      PP:=PROGLOWERB;          {INITIALISE PROGRAM POINTER REGISTER}
      CPUSTATE:=RUNNING;       {INITIALISE PL/T CPU "STATE"}

      REPEAT {INSTRUCTION PROCESSING CYCLE}
      BEGIN TRACEVALID:=(PP >= TRACLOWERB) AND (PP <= TRACUPPERB);
           IF TRACEWANTED AND TRACEVALID THEN
           BEGIN PRINTMCODE(PP); PRINTNL
           END;
           IR:=MEMORY[PP]; PP:=PP+1; {FETCH INSTRUCTION AND INCREMENT PP}
           FUN:=IR DIV 4096; ARG:=IR MOD 4096; {DECODE INSTRUCTION}

           CASE FUN OF          {EXECUTE INSTRUCTION}
        0: BEGIN IF SB+SP = MAXADDRESS THEN
   {LIT}        BEGIN PRINTNL; PRINTLN('STACK OVERFLOW ERROR'); PRINTNL;
                     CPUSTATE:=HALTED
                END
                ELSE
                BEGIN SP:=SP+1; MEMORY[SB+SP]:=ARG
                END
           END;

        1: BEGIN IF SB+SP = MAXADDRESS THEN
   {LOD}        BEGIN PRINTNL; PRINTLN('STACK OVERFLOW ERROR'); PRINTNL;
                     CPUSTATE:=HALTED
                END
                ELSE
                BEGIN SP:=SP+1; MEMORY[SB+SP]:=MEMORY[SB+ARG]
                END
           END;
```

```
  2: BEGIN MEMORY[SB+ARG]:=MEMORY[SB+SP]; SP:=SP-1;
{STO}       PRINTVARIABLE(ARG); PRINTNL
      END;

  3: BEGIN IF ARG <> Ø THEN SP:=SP-1;
{OPR}       CASE ARG OF
        Ø: BEGIN MEMORY[SB+SP]:= -MEMORY[SB+SP]
      {NEG} END;
        1: BEGIN MEMORY[SB+SP]:=MEMORY[SB+SP] + MEMORY[SB+SP+1]
      {ADD} END;
        2: BEGIN MEMORY[SB+SP]:=MEMORY[SB+SP] - MEMORY[SB+SP+1]
      {SUB} END;
        3: BEGIN MEMORY[SB+SP]:=MEMORY[SB+SP] * MEMORY[SB+SP+1]
      {MPY} END;
        4: BEGIN IF MEMORY[SB+SP+1] = Ø THEN
      {DVD} BEGIN PRINTNL; PRINTLN('DIVIDE BY ZERO ERROR'); PRINTNL;
                  CPUSTATE:=HALTED
            END
            ELSE  MEMORY[SB+SP]:=MEMORY[SB+SP] DIV MEMORY[SB+SP+1]
            END;
        5: BEGIN MEMORY[SB+SP]:=ORD(MEMORY[SB+SP] = MEMORY[SB+SP+1])
    {CMPEQL} END;
        6: BEGIN MEMORY[SB+SP]:=ORD(MEMORY[SB+SP] <> MEMORY[SB+SP+1])
    {CMPNEQ} END;
        7: BEGIN MEMORY[SB+SP]:=ORD(MEMORY[SB+SP] < MEMORY[SB+SP+1])
    {CMPLSS} END;
        8: BEGIN MEMORY[SB+SP]:=ORD(MEMORY[SB+SP] <= MEMORY[SB+SP+1])
    {CMPLEQ} END;
        9: BEGIN MEMORY[SB+SP]:=ORD(MEMORY[SB+SP] > MEMORY[SB+SP+1])
    {CMPGTR} END;
       10: BEGIN MEMORY[SB+SP]:=ORD(MEMORY[SB+SP] >= MEMORY[SB+SP+1])
    {CMPGEQ} END
            END {CASE}
      END;

  4: BEGIN PP:=ARG
{JMP} END;

  5: BEGIN IF MEMORY[SB+SP] = Ø THEN PP:=ARG; SP:=SP-1
{JPF} END;

  6: BEGIN CPUSTATE:=HALTED
{HLT} END
      END {CASE};

      IF TRACEWANTED AND TRACEVALID THEN
      BEGIN PRINTREGISTERS; PRINTNL; PRINTNL
      END
END
UNTIL CPUSTATE = HALTED;

WRITELN('EXECUTION HALTED AT @',PP:1);
WRITELN(OUTPUTFILE,'EXECUTION HALTED AT @',PP:1)

END {INTERPRET - PL/T: MACHINE CODE PROGRAM INTERPRETATION};
```

Chapter 13

PARSER
System Program Listing

```
(*$A-*)
PROGRAM PARSER;                 {PL/T: SYNTAX CHECKING WITH ERROR RECOVERY}


{!!!! DATA DEFINITIONS !!!!}


CONST IDENTMAXSIZE = 8;         {MAX. SIGNIFICANT LENGTH OF IDENTIFIERS}
      NUMBRMAXSIZE = 5;         {MAX. NO. OF DIGITS IN NUMBERS}
      MAXIMUMNUMBR = 32767;     {MAX. NUMERICAL VALUE}
      MAXCHARCODE  = 255;       {MAX. CHARACTER CODE VALUE}
      MAXLINESIZE  = 255;       {MAX. SOURCE LINE LENGTH}
      NOOFRESWRDS  = 8;         {NO. OF PL/T RESERVED WORDS}
      RESWRDLIMIT  = 9;         {MAX. BOUND ON RESERVED WORD SEARCH}
      IDTABMAXSIZE = 50;        {MAX. SIZE OF IDENTIFIER TABLE}
      NOOFERRMESGS = 27;        {NO. OF ERROR MESSAGES}
      NULLFILENAME = '!PLTNULL';    {NAME OF NULL OUTPUT FILE}


TYPE  IDSTRING = STRING[IDENTMAXSIZE];     {IDENTIFIER CHARACTER STRING}
      IDKIND   = (CONSTANT,VARIABLE);      {POSSIBLE KINDS OF IDENTIFIER}
      NUMBRVALUE = 0..MAXIMUMNUMBR;        {UNSIGNED NUMERICAL VALUE}
      RESWRDNUMBER = 1..NOOFRESWRDS;       {RESERVED WORD NUMBER}
      IDENTNUMBER  = 0..IDTABMAXSIZE;      {IDENTIFIER TABLE ENTRY NUMBER}
      ERRORNUMBER  = 1..NOOFERRMESGS;      {ERROR/ERROR MESSAGE NUMBER}
      MESSAGETEXT  = STRING[80];           {ERROR/OTHER MESSAGE TEXT}
      ERRORS    = SET OF ERRORNUMBER;
      {POSSIBLE KINDS OF SYMBOL, I.E. LEXICAL TOKENS}
      SYMBOL   = (NUL, IDENT, NUMBR, PLUS, MINUS, TIMES, SLASH,
                  EQL, NEQ, LSS, LEQ, GTR, GEQ, BECOMES,
                  LPAREN, RPAREN, COMMA, SEMICOLON, PERIOD,
                  CONSTSYM, VARSYM, BEGINSYM, ENDSYM,
                  IFSYM, THENSYM, WHILESYM, DOSYM);
      SYMBOLS  = SET OF SYMBOL;


VAR   SOURCEFILE, OUTPUTFILE: TEXT;       {SOURCE AND OUTPUT FILES}
      SOURCENAME, OUTPUTNAME: STRING[20]; {SOURCE AND OUTPUT FILE NAMES}

      SOURCELINE: STRING[MAXLINESIZE];    {CURRENT SOURCE LINE}
      LINELENGTH: 0..MAXLINESIZE;    {LENGTH OF CURRENT SOURCE LINE}
      LINEPTR: 0..MAXLINESIZE;       {CURRENT POSITION WITHIN SOURCE LINE}
      SYMPTR: 0..MAXLINESIZE;        {START OF MOST RECENTLY RECOGNISED SYMBOL}

      CH: CHAR;              {MOST RECENTLY RECOGNISED CHARACTER}
      SYM: SYMBOL;           {MOST RECENTLY RECOGNISED SYMBOL}
      ID: IDSTRING;          {MOST RECENTLY RECOGNISED IDENTIFIER}
      NUM: NUMBRVALUE;       {MOST RECENTLY RECOGNISED NUMBER}

      CHARSYMS: ARRAY[CHAR] OF SYMBOL;     {SYMBOLS FOR INDIVIDUAL CHARACTERS}
      RESWRDS: ARRAY[RESWRDNUMBER] OF IDSTRING;     {RESERVED WORD LIST}
      RESWRDSYMS: ARRAY[RESWRDNUMBER] OF SYMBOL;    {SYMBOLS FOR RESERVED WORDS}

      IDTABLE: ARRAY[IDENTNUMBER] OF       {IDENTIFIER TABLE}
               RECORD NAME: IDSTRING;      {IDENTIFIER NAME}
                      KIND: IDKIND         {IDENTIFIER KIND}
               END;
      IDCOUNT: IDENTNUMBER;                {IDENTIFIER TABLE ENTRY COUNT}

      ERRMESGS: ARRAY[ERRORNUMBER] OF MESSAGETEXT;  {ERROR MESSAGE LIST}
      LINEERRORS, PROGERRORS: ERRORS;      {PER LINE/PROGRAM ERROR NUMBER SETS}
      PERLINEERRMESGS: BOOLEAN;         {PER LINE ERROR MESSAGES? (USER OPTION)}
```

```
{!!!! INITIALISATION, PRINTOUT AND ERROR HANDLING ROUTINES !!!!}

PROCEDURE INITIALISE;                    {INITIALISES GLOBAL VARIABLES}

   PROCEDURE INITSYMBOLS;                {INITIALISES CHARSYMS AND RESWRDS/SYMS}

   VAR   ICH: CHAR;

   BEGIN {INITIALISE SYMBOLS FOR INDIVIDUAL CHARACTERS}
         FOR ICH:=CHR(0) TO CHR(MAXCHARCODE) DO CHARSYMS[ICH]:=NUL;
         CHARSYMS['+']:=PLUS;  CHARSYMS['-']:=MINUS;     CHARSYMS['*']:=TIMES;
         CHARSYMS['/']:=SLASH; CHARSYMS['(']:=LPAREN;    CHARSYMS[')']:=RPAREN;
         CHARSYMS['=']:=EQL;   CHARSYMS['<']:=LSS;       CHARSYMS['>']:=GTR;
         CHARSYMS[',']:=COMMA; CHARSYMS[';']:=SEMICOLON; CHARSYMS['.']:=PERIOD;

         {INITIALISE RESERVED WORD AND ASSOCIATED SYMBOL LISTS, ALPHABETICALLY}
         RESWRDS[1]:='BEGIN   ';   RESWRDSYMS[1]:=BEGINSYM;
         RESWRDS[2]:='CONST   ';   RESWRDSYMS[2]:=CONSTSYM;
         RESWRDS[3]:='DO      ';   RESWRDSYMS[3]:=DOSYM;
         RESWRDS[4]:='END     ';   RESWRDSYMS[4]:=ENDSYM;
         RESWRDS[5]:='IF      ';   RESWRDSYMS[5]:=IFSYM;
         RESWRDS[6]:='THEN    ';   RESWRDSYMS[6]:=THENSYM;
         RESWRDS[7]:='VAR     ';   RESWRDSYMS[7]:=VARSYM;
         RESWRDS[8]:='WHILE   ';   RESWRDSYMS[8]:=WHILESYM
   END {INITSYMBOLS};

   PROCEDURE INITERRMESGS;              {INITIALISES ERROR MESSAGE LIST}
   BEGIN ERRMESGS[1] :='("CONST" OR) "VAR" DECLARATION(S) EXPECTED.';
         ERRMESGS[2] :='"=" MUST BE FOLLOWED BY A NUMBER.';
         ERRMESGS[3] :='IDENTIFIER MUST BE FOLLOWED BY "=".';
         ERRMESGS[4] :='"CONST" OR "VAR" MUST BE FOLLOWED BY AN IDENTIFIER.';
         ERRMESGS[5] :='SEMICOLON OR COMMA MISSING.';
         ERRMESGS[6] :='WRONG SYMBOL FOLLOWING IDENTIFIER DECLARATION.';
         ERRMESGS[7] :='STATEMENT EXPECTED.';
         ERRMESGS[8] :='WRONG SYMBOL FOLLOWING STATEMENT PART OF BLOCK.';
         ERRMESGS[9] :='FULL STOP EXPECTED.';
         ERRMESGS[10]:='SEMICOLON MISSING BETWEEN STATEMENTS.';
         ERRMESGS[11]:='UNDECLARED IDENTIFIER.';
         ERRMESGS[12]:='ASSIGNMENT TO CONSTANT IS NOT ALLOWED.';
         ERRMESGS[13]:='ASSIGNMENT OPERATOR ":=" EXPECTED.';
         ERRMESGS[14]:='SYSTEM FAULT - PLEASE REPORT TO TUTOR.';
         ERRMESGS[15]:=ERRMESGS[14];
         ERRMESGS[16]:='"THEN" EXPECTED.';
         ERRMESGS[17]:='SEMICOLON OR "END" EXPECTED.';
         ERRMESGS[18]:='"DO" EXPECTED.';
         ERRMESGS[19]:='WRONG SYMBOL FOLLOWING STATEMENT.';
         ERRMESGS[20]:='RELATIONAL OPERATOR EXPECTED.';
         ERRMESGS[21]:=ERRMESGS[14];
         ERRMESGS[22]:='RIGHT PARENTHESIS MISSING.';
         ERRMESGS[23]:='IDENTIFIER, NUMBER OR "(" EXPECTED.';
         ERRMESGS[24]:='WRONG SYMBOL FOLLOWING FACTOR.';
         ERRMESGS[25]:='NUMBER TOO LARGE.';
         ERRMESGS[26]:='IDENTIFIER TABLE OVERFLOW.';
         ERRMESGS[27]:='SOURCE PROGRAM INCOMPLETE.'
   END {INITERRMESGS};
```

```
BEGIN {INITIALISE SYMBOLS, IDENTIFIER TABLE AND ERROR MESSAGE LIST}
      INITSYMBOLS;          IDCOUNT:=0;           INITERRMESGS;

      {INITIALISE PER LINE/PER PROGRAM ERROR NUMBER SETS}
      LINEERRORS:=[];      PROGERRORS:=[];

      {INITIALISE LEXICAL STATE VARIABLES}
      LINELENGTH:=0; LINEPTR:=0; SYMPTR:=0; CH:=' '
END {INITIALISE};

PROCEDURE PRINTLN(MESG: MESSAGETEXT);   {WRITES MESSAGE LINE TO SCREEN AND FILE}
BEGIN WRITELN(MESG); WRITELN(OUTPUTFILE,MESG)
END {PRINTLN};

PROCEDURE PRINTNL;                       {WRITES BLANK LINE TO SCREEN AND FILE}
BEGIN WRITELN; WRITELN(OUTPUTFILE)
END {PRINTNL};

PROCEDURE PRINTABORT(EN: ERRORNUMBER); {WRITES "DISASTROUS" ERROR MESSAGE TO
                                        SCREEN AND FILE, THEN ABORTS PARSING}
BEGIN PRINTNL; PRINTLN(ERRMESGS[EN]);

      CLOSE(SOURCEFILE);

      PRINTNL; PRINTNL;
      PRINTLN('^^^^^^^^^^^^^^^^^^^^^^^^^^^^^^');
      PRINTLN('^ SYNTAX CHECKING ABORTED. ^');
      PRINTLN('^^^^^^^^^^^^^^^^^^^^^^^^^^^^^^');
      PRINTNL; PRINTNL;

      CLOSE(OUTPUTFILE);
      IF OUTPUTNAME = NULLFILENAME THEN ERASE(OUTPUTFILE)
      ELSE WRITELN('(SEE ',CONCAT(OUTPUTNAME,'.LST'),' FOR OUTPUT.)');
      WRITELN;

      HALT
END {PRINTABORT};

PROCEDURE MARKERROR(EN: ERRORNUMBER);   {RECORDS ERROR OCCURRENCE, AND WRITES
                                        "POSITIONAL" ERROR NUMBER LINE
                                        (WITHOUT MESSAGE) TO SCREEN AND FILE}
BEGIN LINEERRORS:=LINEERRORS+[EN]; PROGERRORS:=PROGERRORS+[EN];
      WRITELN(' ':SYMPTR,'^',EN:1); WRITELN(OUTPUTFILE,' ':SYMPTR,'^',EN:1)
END {MARKERROR};

PROCEDURE PRINTERRMESG(EN: ERRORNUMBER); {WRITES "NUMBERED" ERROR MESSAGE
                                        SUMMARY LINE TO SCREEN AND FILE}
BEGIN WRITELN(EN:2,': ',ERRMESGS[EN]);
      WRITELN(OUTPUTFILE,EN:2,': ',ERRMESGS[EN])
END {PRINTERRMESG};
```

```
PROCEDURE PRINTLINEERRMESGS;              {PRINTS PER LINE ERROR MESSAGE SUMMARY}

VAR    EN: ERRORNUMBER;

BEGIN IF LINEERRORS <> [] THEN
      BEGIN FOR EN:=1 TO NOOFERRMESGS DO
            IF EN IN LINEERRORS THEN PRINTERRMESG(EN);
            LINEERRORS:=[];
            PRINTNL
      END
END {PRINTLINEERRMESGS};

PROCEDURE PRINTPROGERRMESGS;              {PRINTS PROGRAM ERROR MESSAGE SUMMARY}

VAR    EN:ERRORNUMBER;

BEGIN PRINTNL; PRINTNL;
      IF PROGERRORS <> [] THEN
      BEGIN PRINTLN('ERROR SUMMARY:-');
            PRINTLN('===============');
            FOR EN:=1 TO NOOFERRMESGS DO
            IF EN IN PROGERRORS THEN PRINTERRMESG(EN);
            PROGERRORS:=[]
      END
      ELSE
      BEGIN PRINTLN('NO ERRORS FOUND');
            PRINTLN('===============')
      END;
      PRINTNL; PRINTNL
END {PRINTPROGERRMESGS};

PROCEDURE GETSYM; FORWARD;

PROCEDURE CHECKSYM(GOALSYMS, CONTEXT: SYMBOLS; EN: ERRORNUMBER);
{CHECKS FOR SYNTAX ERRORS, RE-SYNCHRONISING SOURCE INPUT AS NECESSARY}
BEGIN IF NOT (SYM IN GOALSYMS) THEN
      BEGIN MARKERROR(EN);
            GOALSYMS:=GOALSYMS+CONTEXT;
            WHILE NOT (SYM IN GOALSYMS) DO GETSYM
      END
END {CHECKSYM};

PROCEDURE OPTIONDIALOGUE;                 {DETERMINES USER OPTION SETTINGS}

VAR    ANSWERCH: CHAR;

BEGIN WRITELN('DO YOU WANT ERROR MESSAGES (BESIDES NUMBERS) AFTER EACH LINE?');
      WRITE('ANSWER Y(ES) IF YOU DO, OTHERWISE NO WILL BE ASSUMED: ');
      READLN(ANSWERCH); WRITELN;
      IF ANSWERCH = 'Y' THEN PERLINEERRMESGS:=TRUE ELSE PERLINEERRMESGS:=FALSE
END {OPTIONDIALOGUE};
```

{ ¦¦¦¦ LEXICAL ANALYSIS (SYMBOL RECOGNITION) ROUTINES ¦¦¦¦}

```
PROCEDURE GETSYM;                        {GETS NEXT SOURCE PROGRAM SYMBOL}

VAR    SIZE: 0..MAXLINESIZE; LOWER, MIDDLE, UPPER: 0..RESWRDLIMIT; DIGIT: 0..9;

    PROCEDURE GETCH;                     {GETS NEXT SOURCE PROGRAM CHARACTER}
    BEGIN IF LINEPTR = LINELENGTH THEN   {AT END OF CURRENT SOURCE LINE}
        BEGIN IF PERLINEERRMESGS THEN PRINTLINEERRMESGS;

            IF EOF(SOURCEFILE) THEN PRINTABORT(27);

            {READ, PRINT AND INITIALISE NEXT SOURCE LINE}
            WRITE(' '); WRITE(OUTPUTFILE,' ');
            READLN(SOURCEFILE,SOURCELINE); PRINTLN(SOURCELINE);
            LINELENGTH:=LENGTH(SOURCELINE); LINEPTR:=0; SYMPTR:=1;

            {COMPENSATE FOR ONE CHARACTER LOOKAHEAD AT END OF LINE}
            SOURCELINE:=CONCAT(SOURCELINE,' '); LINELENGTH:=LINELENGTH+1
        END;

        {GET NEXT CHARACTER FROM CURRENT SOURCE LINE}
        LINEPTR:=LINEPTR+1; CH:=SOURCELINE[LINEPTR]
    END {GETCH};

BEGIN {GETSYM}
    WHILE CH = ' ' DO GETCH;             {IGNORE ANY SPACES BEFORE NEXT SYMBOL}

    WHILE CH = '{' DO                    {IGNORE ANY COMMENTARY SIMILARLY}
    BEGIN REPEAT GETCH UNTIL CH = '}'; REPEAT GETCH UNTIL CH <> ' '
    END;

    SYMPTR:=LINEPTR;                     {RECORD START OF SYMBOL}
    IF CH IN ['A'..'Z'] THEN
    BEGIN {IDENTIFIER OR RESERVED WORD}
        ID:='        '; SIZE:=0;
        REPEAT {COLLECT IDENTIFIER CHARACTERS IN ID}
        BEGIN IF SIZE < IDENTMAXSIZE THEN
            BEGIN SIZE:=SIZE+1; ID[SIZE]:=CH
            END;
            GETCH
        END
        UNTIL NOT (CH IN ['A'..'Z','0'..'9']);

        {BINARY SEARCH RESERVED WORD LIST FOR ID}
        LOWER:=1; UPPER:=NOOFRESWRDS;
        REPEAT
        BEGIN MIDDLE:=(LOWER+UPPER) DIV 2;
            IF ID <= RESWRDS[MIDDLE] THEN UPPER:= MIDDLE-1;
            IF ID >= RESWRDS[MIDDLE] THEN LOWER:= MIDDLE+1
        END
        UNTIL LOWER > UPPER;

        {SYMBOL IS IDENTIFIER OR APPROPRIATE RESERVED WORD SYMBOL}
        IF ID = RESWRDS[MIDDLE] THEN SYM:=RESWRDSYMS[MIDDLE]
        ELSE SYM:=IDENT
    END
```

```
      ELSE
      IF CH IN ['0'..'9'] THEN
      BEGIN {NUMBER}
            SYM:=NUMBR;
            NUM:=0; SIZE:=0;
            REPEAT {ACCUMULATE VALUE OF NUMBER IN NUM}
            BEGIN SIZE:=SIZE+1; DIGIT:=ORD(CH)-ORD('0');
                  IF SIZE = NUMBRMAXSIZE THEN {CHECK FOR OVERFLOW}
                  BEGIN IF NUM > (MAXIMUMNUMBR-DIGIT) DIV 10 THEN MARKERROR(25)
                        ELSE NUM:=10*NUM+DIGIT
                  END
                  ELSE
                  IF SIZE < NUMBRMAXSIZE THEN NUM:=10*NUM+DIGIT;
                  GETCH
            END
            UNTIL NOT (CH IN ['0'..'9']);
            IF SIZE > NUMBRMAXSIZE THEN MARKERROR(25)
      END
      ELSE
      IF CH = ':' THEN
      BEGIN {POSSIBLY ':='}
            GETCH;
            IF CH = '=' THEN
            BEGIN SYM:=BECOMES; GETCH
            END
            ELSE SYM:=NUL
      END
      ELSE
      IF CH = '<' THEN
      BEGIN {'<', '<=' OR '<>'}
            GETCH;
            IF CH = '=' THEN
            BEGIN SYM:=LEQ; GETCH
            END
            ELSE
            IF CH = '>' THEN
            BEGIN SYM:=NEQ; GETCH
            END
            ELSE SYM:=LSS
      END
      ELSE
      IF CH = '>' THEN
      BEGIN {'>' OR '>='}
            GETCH;
            IF CH = '=' THEN
            BEGIN SYM:=GEQ; GETCH
            END
            ELSE SYM:=GTR
      END
      ELSE {FOR ALL OTHER CHARACTERS,
            E.G. '+', '-', '*', '/', '(', ')', '=', ',', ';', '.'}
      BEGIN SYM:=CHARSYMS[CH]; GETCH
      END
END {GETSYM};
```

```
{!!!! SYNTAX ANALYSIS (PARSING) ROUTINES !!!!}

PROCEDURE BLOCK(CONTEXT: SYMBOLS);

    PROCEDURE ENTERID(ID: IDSTRING; IK: IDKIND); {ENTER ID IN IDENTIFIER TABLE}
    BEGIN IF IDCOUNT = IDTABMAXSIZE THEN PRINTABORT(26);
         IDCOUNT:=IDCOUNT+1;
         WITH IDTABLE[IDCOUNT] DO
         BEGIN NAME:=ID; KIND:=IK
         END
    END {ENTERID};

    FUNCTION LOOKUPID(ID: IDSTRING): IDENTNUMBER; {LOOK UP ENTRY NUMBER OF
                                                   ID IN IDENTIFIER TABLE;
                                                   RETURN 0 IF NOT PRESENT}

    VAR   IEN: IDENTNUMBER;

    BEGIN IDTABLE[0].NAME:=ID;
         IEN:=IDCOUNT;
         WHILE IDTABLE[IEN].NAME <> ID DO IEN:=IEN-1; {BACKWARDS TABLE SEARCH}
         LOOKUPID:=IEN
    END {LOOKUPID};

    PROCEDURE CONSTDECLARATION(CONTEXT: SYMBOLS);
    BEGIN (* <CONSTDECLARATION> ::= IDENT = NUMBR *)
         CHECKSYM([IDENT],CONTEXT,4);
         WHILE SYM = IDENT DO
         BEGIN GETSYM;
              IF SYM = EQL THEN
              BEGIN GETSYM;
                   IF SYM = NUMBR THEN
                   BEGIN ENTERID(ID,CONSTANT);
                        GETSYM
                   END
                   ELSE MARKERROR(2)
              END
              ELSE MARKERROR(3);
              CHECKSYM(CONTEXT,[IDENT],6)
         END
    END {CONSTDECLARATION};

    PROCEDURE VARDECLARATION(CONTEXT: SYMBOLS);
    BEGIN (* <VARDECLARATION> ::= IDENT *)
         CHECKSYM([IDENT],CONTEXT,4);
         WHILE SYM = IDENT DO
         BEGIN ENTERID(ID,VARIABLE);
              GETSYM;
              CHECKSYM(CONTEXT,[IDENT],6)
         END
    END {VARDECLARATION};
```

```
PROCEDURE STATEMENT(CONTEXT: SYMBOLS);

VAR   INDEX: IDENTNUMBER;

  PROCEDURE EXPRESSION(CONTEXT: SYMBOLS);

    PROCEDURE TERM(CONTEXT: SYMBOLS);

        PROCEDURE FACTOR(CONTEXT: SYMBOLS);
        BEGIN (* <FACTOR> ::= IDENT | NUMBR | ( <EXPRESSION> ) *)
            CHECKSYM([IDENT,NUMBR,LPAREN],CONTEXT,23);
            WHILE SYM IN [IDENT,NUMBR,LPAREN] DO
            BEGIN IF SYM = IDENT THEN
                BEGIN IF LOOKUPID(ID) = 0 THEN MARKERROR(11);
                     GETSYM
                END
                ELSE
                IF SYM = NUMBR THEN
                BEGIN GETSYM
                END
                ELSE
                IF SYM = LPAREN THEN
                BEGIN GETSYM; EXPRESSION([RPAREN]+CONTEXT);
                     IF SYM = RPAREN THEN GETSYM ELSE MARKERROR(22)
                END;
                CHECKSYM(CONTEXT,[LPAREN],24)
            END
        END {FACTOR};

    BEGIN (* <TERM> ::= <FACTOR> {(*|/) <FACTOR>} *)·
        FACTOR(CONTEXT+[TIMES,SLASH]);
        WHILE SYM IN [TIMES,SLASH] DO
        BEGIN GETSYM; FACTOR(CONTEXT+[TIMES,SLASH])
        END
    END {TERM};

  BEGIN (* <EXPRESSION> ::= [(+|-)] <TERM> {(+|-) <TERM>} *)
      IF SYM IN [PLUS,MINUS] THEN GETSYM;
      TERM(CONTEXT+[PLUS,MINUS]);
      WHILE SYM IN [PLUS,MINUS] DO
      BEGIN GETSYM; TERM(CONTEXT+[PLUS,MINUS])
      END
  END {EXPRESSION};

  PROCEDURE CONDITION(CONTEXT: SYMBOLS);
  BEGIN (* <CONDITION> ::= <EXPRESSION> (=|<>|<|<=|>|>=) <EXPRESSION> *)
      EXPRESSION([EQL,NEQ,LSS,LEQ,GTR,GEQ]+CONTEXT);
      IF SYM IN [EQL,NEQ,LSS,LEQ,GTR,GEQ] THEN
      BEGIN GETSYM; EXPRESSION(CONTEXT)
      END
      ELSE MARKERROR(20)
  END {CONDITION};
```

```
BEGIN {STATEMENT}
      CHECKSYM([IDENT,IFSYM,BEGINSYM,WHILESYM],CONTEXT,7);
      IF SYM = IDENT THEN
      BEGIN (* <STATEMENT> ::= IDENT := <EXPRESSION> *)
            INDEX:=LOOKUPID(ID);
            IF INDEX = Ø THEN MARKERROR(11)
            ELSE
            IF IDTABLE[INDEX].KIND <> VARIABLE THEN MARKERROR(12);
            GETSYM;
            IF SYM = BECOMES THEN GETSYM ELSE MARKERROR(13);
            EXPRESSION(CONTEXT)
      END
      ELSE
      IF SYM = IFSYM THEN
      BEGIN (* <STATEMENT> ::= IF <CONDITION> THEN <STATEMENT> *)
            GETSYM; CONDITION([THENSYM,DOSYM]+CONTEXT);
            IF SYM = THENSYM THEN GETSYM ELSE MARKERROR(16);
            STATEMENT(CONTEXT)
      END
      ELSE
      IF SYM = BEGINSYM THEN
      BEGIN (* <STATEMENT> ::= BEGIN <STATEMENT> {; <STATEMENT>} END *)
            GETSYM; STATEMENT([SEMICOLON,ENDSYM]+CONTEXT);
            WHILE SYM IN [SEMICOLON]+[IFSYM,BEGINSYM,WHILESYM] DO
            BEGIN IF SYM = SEMICOLON THEN GETSYM ELSE MARKERROR(10);
                  STATEMENT([SEMICOLON,ENDSYM]+CONTEXT)
            END;
            IF SYM = ENDSYM THEN GETSYM ELSE MARKERROR(17)
      END
      ELSE
      IF SYM = WHILESYM THEN
      BEGIN (* <STATEMENT> ::= WHILE <CONDITION> DO <STATEMENT> *)
            GETSYM; CONDITION([DOSYM]+CONTEXT);
            IF SYM = DOSYM THEN GETSYM ELSE MARKERROR(18);
            STATEMENT(CONTEXT)
      END;
      CHECKSYM(CONTEXT,[],19)
END {STATEMENT};
```

```
BEGIN (* <BLOCK> ::= [CONST <CONSTDECLARATION> {, <CONSTDECLARATION>} ;]
                     VAR <VARDECLARATION> {, <VARDECLARATION>} ;
                     <STATEMENT>                                              *)
      CONTEXT:=CONTEXT+[CONSTSYM,VARSYM]+[IFSYM,WHILESYM,BEGINSYM];
      CHECKSYM([CONSTSYM,VARSYM],CONTEXT,1);
      WHILE SYM = CONSTSYM DO
      BEGIN GETSYM; CONSTDECLARATION([COMMA,SEMICOLON]+CONTEXT);
            WHILE SYM = COMMA DO
            BEGIN GETSYM; CONSTDECLARATION([COMMA,SEMICOLON]+CONTEXT)
            END;
            IF SYM = SEMICOLON THEN GETSYM ELSE MARKERROR(5)
      END;
      CHECKSYM([VARSYM],CONTEXT,1);
      WHILE SYM = VARSYM DO
      BEGIN GETSYM; VARDECLARATION([COMMA,SEMICOLON]+CONTEXT);
            WHILE SYM = COMMA DO
            BEGIN GETSYM; VARDECLARATION([COMMA,SEMICOLON]+CONTEXT)
            END;
            IF SYM = SEMICOLON THEN GETSYM ELSE MARKERROR(5)
      END;
      STATEMENT([SEMICOLON,ENDSYM]+CONTEXT);
      CHECKSYM(CONTEXT,[SEMICOLON,ENDSYM],8)
END {BLOCK};
```

```
{!!!! MAIN PROGRAM !!!!}

BEGIN {PARSER - PL/T: SYNTAX CHECKING WITH ERROR RECOVERY}
      INITIALISE;

      WRITELN; WRITELN;
      WRITELN('PL/T: SYNTAX CHECKING WITH ERROR RECOVERY.');
      WRITELN('****************************************');
      WRITELN; WRITELN;

      WRITE('PLEASE TYPE IN NAME OF PL/T SOURCE CODE TEXT FILE: ');
      READLN(SOURCENAME);
      ASSIGN(SOURCEFILE,CONCAT(SOURCENAME,'.PLT')); RESET(SOURCEFILE);
      WRITELN;

      WRITE('PLEASE TYPE IN NAME OF OUTPUT LIST FILE ("RETURN" FOR NONE): ');
      READLN(OUTPUTNAME);
      IF OUTPUTNAME = '' THEN OUTPUTNAME:=NULLFILENAME;
      ASSIGN(OUTPUTFILE,CONCAT(OUTPUTNAME,'.LST')); REWRITE(OUTPUTFILE);
      WRITELN;

      WRITELN(OUTPUTFILE); WRITELN(OUTPUTFILE);
      WRITELN(OUTPUTFILE,'PL/T: SYNTAX CHECKING WITH ERROR RECOVERY.');
      WRITELN(OUTPUTFILE,'****************************************');
      WRITELN(OUTPUTFILE); WRITELN(OUTPUTFILE);
      WRITELN(OUTPUTFILE,'PL/T SOURCE FILE WAS ',CONCAT(SOURCENAME,'.PLT'));
      WRITELN(OUTPUTFILE);

      OPTIONDIALOGUE; {GET THE USER TO SPECIFY HIS OPTIONS}

      PRINTNL; PRINTNL;
      PRINTLN('^^^^^^^^^^^^^^^^^^^^^^^^^^^^^^^^^^^');
      PRINTLN('^ SYNTAX CHECKING STARTS NOW: ^');
      PRINTLN('^^^^^^^^^^^^^^^^^^^^^^^^^^^^^^^^^^^');
      PRINTNL; PRINTNL;

      GETSYM;          {GET NEXT (I.E. FIRST) SOURCE SYMBOL}
      (* <PROGRAM> ::= <BLOCK> . *)
      BLOCK([PERIOD]); {ATTEMPT TO PARSE A BLOCK}
      IF SYM <> PERIOD THEN MARKERROR(9);
      IF PERLINEERRMESGS THEN PRINTLINEERRMESGS;

      PRINTPROGERRMESGS; {PRINT ERROR MESSAGE SUMMARY FOR PROGRAM}

      CLOSE(SOURCEFILE);

      PRINTNL; PRINTNL;
      PRINTLN('^^^^^^^^^^^^^^^^^^^^^^^^^^^^^^^^^^^');
      PRINTLN('^ SYNTAX CHECKING COMPLETED. ^');
      PRINTLN('^^^^^^^^^^^^^^^^^^^^^^^^^^^^^^^^^^^');
      PRINTNL; PRINTNL;

      CLOSE(OUTPUTFILE);
      IF OUTPUTNAME = NULLFILENAME THEN ERASE(OUTPUTFILE)
      ELSE WRITELN('(SEE ',CONCAT(OUTPUTNAME,'.LST'),' FOR OUTPUT.)');
      WRITELN
 END {PARSER - PL/T: SYNTAX CHECKING WITH ERROR RECOVERY}.
```

Appendix

PL/T Sample Program Compilation
and Execution Listings

Appendix 1. PL/T sample program with identifier/machine language summaries

{A PL/T PROGRAM TO COUNT DIGITS IN A NUMBER}

```
CONST RADIX=10;
VAR   NUMBER,DCOUNT;

BEGIN NUMBER:=0; {SIMULATE INPUT OF NUMBER BY ASSIGNMENT}
      DCOUNT:=0; {INITIALISE DIGIT COUNT}
      IF NUMBER=0 THEN DCOUNT:=1; {NUMBER 0 IS A SPECIAL CASE}
      WHILE NUMBER<>0 DO {LOOP TO COUNT DIGITS WHILE ANY LEFT}
      BEGIN NUMBER:=NUMBER/RADIX; DCOUNT:=DCOUNT+1
      END
      {DCOUNT CONTAINS THE DESIRED RESULT}
END.
```

```
IDENTIFIERS SUMMARY:-
=====================
->      RADIX   = 10
->      NUMBER  =@S[0]
->      DCOUNT  =@S[1]
```

```
MACHINE CODE SUMMARY:-
======================
->@  0: (#0000#)    LIT    0
->@  1: (#2000#)    STO    @S[0]
->@  2: (#0000#)    LIT    0
->@  3: (#2001#)    STO    @S[1]
->@  4: (#1000#)    LOD    @S[0]
->@  5: (#0000#)    LIT    0
->@  6: (#3005#)    OPR    5    {CMPEQL}
->@  7: (#500A#)    JPF    @10
->@  8: (#0001#)    LIT    1
->@  9: (#2001#)    STO    @S[1]
->@ 10: (#1000#)    LOD    @S[0]
->@ 11: (#0000#)    LIT    0
->@ 12: (#3006#)    OPR    6    {CMPNEQ}
->@ 13: (#5017#)    JPF    @23
->@ 14: (#1000#)    LOD    @S[0]
->@ 15: (#000A#)    LIT    10
->@ 16: (#3004#)    OPR    4    {DVD}
->@ 17: (#2000#)    STO    @S[0]
->@ 18: (#1001#)    LOD    @S[1]
->@ 19: (#0001#)    LIT    1
->@ 20: (#3001#)    OPR    1    {ADD}
->@ 21: (#2001#)    STO    @S[1]
->@ 22: (#400A#)    JMP    @10
->@ 23: (#6000#)    HLT    0
```

64

Appendix 2. PL/T sample program with per-statement machine language and results.

{A PL/T PROGRAM TO COUNT DIGITS IN A NUMBER}

```
CONST RADIX=10;
->       RADIX   = 10

VAR    NUMBER,DCOUNT;
->        NUMBER  =@S[0]
->        DCOUNT  =@S[1]

BEGIN NUMBER:=0; {SIMULATE INPUT OF NUMBER BY ASSIGNMENT}
->@  0: (#0000#)      LIT      0
->@  1: (#2000#)      STO      @S[0]
       DCOUNT:=0; {INITIALISE DIGIT COUNT}
->@  2: (#0000#)      LIT      0
->@  3: (#2001#)      STO      @S[1]

       IF NUMBER=0 THEN DCOUNT:=1; {NUMBER 0 IS A SPECIAL CASE}
->@  4: (#1000#)      LOD      @S[0]
->@  5: (#0000#)      LIT      0
->@  6: (#3005#)      OPR      5    {CMPEQL}
->@  7: (#5000#)      JPF      @0
->@  8: (#0001#)      LIT      1
->@  9: (#2001#)      STO      @S[1]
->@  7: (#500A#)      JPF      @10

       WHILE NUMBER<>0 DO {LOOP TO COUNT DIGITS WHILE ANY LEFT}
->@ 10: (#1000#)      LOD      @S[0]
->@ 11: (#0000#)      LIT      0
->@ 12: (#3006#)      OPR      6    {CMPNEQ}
->@ 13: (#5000#)      JPF      @0

       BEGIN NUMBER:=NUMBER/RADIX; DCOUNT:=DCOUNT+1
->@ 14: (#1000#)      LOD      @S[0]
->@ 15: (#000A#)      LIT      10
->@ 16: (#3004#)      OPR      4    {DVD}
->@ 17: (#2000#)      STO      @S[0]
->@ 18: (#1001#)      LOD      @S[1]
->@ 19: (#0001#)      LIT      1
       END
->@ 20: (#3001#)      OPR      1    {ADD}
->@ 21: (#2001#)      STO      @S[1]

       {DCOUNT CONTAINS THE DESIRED RESULT}
END.
->@ 22: (#400A#)      JMP      @10
->@ 13: (#5017#)      JPF      @23
->@ 23: (#6000#)      HLT      0


VAR RESULTS SUMMARY:-
==========================
@S[0]   NUMBER   :=0
@S[1]   DCOUNT   :=1
```

Appendix 3. PL/T sample program with full execution trace

```
{A PL/T PROGRAM TO COUNT DIGITS IN A NUMBER}

CONST RADIX=1Ø;
VAR    NUMBER,DCOUNT;

BEGIN NUMBER:=Ø; {SIMULATE INPUT OF NUMBER BY ASSIGNMENT}
      DCOUNT:=Ø; {INITIALISE DIGIT COUNT}
      IF NUMBER=Ø THEN DCOUNT:=1; {NUMBER Ø IS A SPECIAL CASE}
      WHILE NUMBER<>Ø DO {LOOP TO COUNT DIGITS WHILE ANY LEFT}
      BEGIN NUMBER:=NUMBER/RADIX; DCOUNT:=DCOUNT+1
      END
      {DCOUNT CONTAINS THE DESIRED RESULT}
END.
```

```
IDENTIFIERS SUMMARY:-
======================
->      RADIX    = 1Ø
->      NUMBER   =@S[Ø]
->      DCOUNT   =@S[1]
```

```
MACHINE CODE SUMMARY:-
======================
->@  Ø: (#ØØØØ#)    LIT     Ø
->@  1: (#2ØØØ#)    STO     @S[Ø]
->@  2: (#ØØØØ#)    LIT     Ø
->@  3: (#2ØØ1#)    STO     @S[1]
->@  4: (#1ØØØ#)    LOD     @S[Ø]
->@  5: (#ØØØØ#)    LIT     Ø
->@  6: (#3ØØ5#)    OPR     5   {CMPEQL}
->@  7: (#5ØØA#)    JPF     @1Ø
->@  8: (#ØØØ1#)    LIT     1
->@  9: (#2ØØ1#)    STO     @S[1]
->@ 1Ø: (#1ØØØ#)    LOD     @S[Ø]
->@ 11: (#ØØØØ#)    LIT     Ø
->@ 12: (#3ØØ6#)    OPR     6   {CMPNEQ}
->@ 13: (#5Ø17#)    JPF     @23
->@ 14: (#1ØØØ#)    LOD     @S[Ø]
->@ 15: (#ØØØA#)    LIT     1Ø
->@ 16: (#3ØØ4#)    OPR     4   {DVD}
->@ 17: (#2ØØØ#)    STO     @S[Ø]
->@ 18: (#1ØØ1#)    LOD     @S[1]
->@ 19: (#ØØØ1#)    LIT     1
->@ 2Ø: (#3ØØ1#)    OPR     1   {ADD}
->@ 21: (#2ØØ1#)    STO     @S[1]
->@ 22: (#4ØØA#)    JMP     @1Ø
->@ 23: (#6ØØØ#)    HLT     Ø
```

```
^^^^^^^^^^^^^^^^^^^^^^^^^^^^^^^^^^^^^^^^^^^^
^ MACHINE CODE EXECUTION STARTS NOW: ^
^^^^^^^^^^^^^^^^^^^^^^^^^^^^^^^^^^^^^^^^^^^^
```

```
->@  0: (#0000#)     LIT     0
PP= 1   SP= 2   S[1]=-32767   S[2]=0


->@  1: (#2000#)     STO     @S[0]
@S[0]   NUMBER  :=0
PP= 2   SP= 1   S[0]=0   S[1]=-32767


->@  2: (#0000#)     LIT     0
PP= 3   SP= 2   S[1]=-32767   S[2]=0


->@  3: (#2001#)     STO     @S[1]
@S[1]   DCOUNT  :=0
PP= 4   SP= 1   S[0]=0   S[1]=0


->@  4: (#1000#)     LOD     @S[0]
PP= 5   SP= 2   S[1]=0   S[2]=0


->@  5: (#0000#)     LIT     0
PP= 6   SP= 3   S[2]=0   S[3]=0


->@  6: (#3005#)      OPR     5   {CMPEQL}
PP= 7   SP= 2   S[1]=0   S[2]=1


->@  7: (#500A#)     JPF     @10
PP= 8   SP= 1   S[0]=0   S[1]=0
```

```
->@  8: (#0001#)      LIT      1

PP= 9   SP= 2   S[1]=0   S[2]=1


->@  9: (#2001#)      STO      @S[1]

@S[1]   DCOUNT  :=1

PP=10   SP= 1   S[0]=0   S[1]=1


->@ 10: (#1000#)      LOD      @S[0]

PP=11   SP= 2   S[1]=1   S[2]=0


->@ 11: (#0000#)      LIT      0

PP=12   SP= 3   S[2]=0   S[3]=0


->@ 12: (#3006#)      OPR      6    {CMPNEQ}

PP=13   SP= 2   S[1]=1   S[2]=0


->@ 13: (#5017#)      JPF      @23

PP=23   SP= 1   S[0]=0   S[1]=1


->@ 23: (#6000#)      HLT      0

PP=24   SP= 1   S[0]=0   S[1]=1


EXECUTION HALTED AT @24


VAR RESULTS SUMMARY:-
=====================
@S[0]   NUMBER  :=0
@S[1]   DCOUNT  :=1


^^^^^^^^^^^^^^^^^^^^^^^^^^^^^^^^^^^^^^^^^^
^ MACHINE CODE EXECUTION COMPLETED.  ^
^^^^^^^^^^^^^^^^^^^^^^^^^^^^^^^^^^^^^^^^^^
```

Exercises

PL/T Programming Exercises

1. Write a PL/T program to determine the largest value of three unordered integer values, allowing for the fact that some or all of the values may be equal; e.g. the largest value of 1, 4, 2 is 4.

2. Write a PL/T program to determine the median (middle) value of three unordered integer values, allowing for the fact that some or all of the values may be equal; e.g. the median of 1, 4, 2 is 2.*

3. Write a PL/T program to compute the sum of the individual decimal digits of a non-negative integer; e.g. the digit sum for 142 is 7.

4. Write a PL/T program to compute the reverse of a non-negative integer considered as a string of decimal digits; e.g. the reverse of 142 is 241.*

5. Write a PL/T program to determine whether or not a non-negative integer is a palindromic number (answer 0 for No, 1 for Yes); e.g. 123 is not palindromic, but 131 is.

6. Write a PL/T program to determine whether or not a non-negative integer is a prime number (answer 0 for No, 1 for Yes); e.g. 123 is not prime, but 131 is.

7. Write a PL/T program to compute the GCD (greatest common divisor) of two positive integers using Euler's method; e.g. the GCD of 12 and 21 is 3.

8. Write a PL/T program to compute the NCR (binomial coefficient) for positive integers N and R ($N \geqslant R$); e.g. the NCR for $N=12$, $R=2$ is 66.*

*Solutions to these exercises are given on page 70.

Solutions

Selected Solutions to
PL/T Programming Exercises

2. ```
{A PL/T PROGRAM TO FIND THE MEDIAN OF THREE VALUES}

VAR A,B,C,T,MEDIAN;

BEGIN {SIMULATE INPUT OF A,B,C BY ASSIGNMENT}
      A:=1; B:=4; C:=2;
      {COMPUTE THE MEDIAN OF A, B AND C}
      IF A>B THEN
      BEGIN T:=A; A:=B; B:=T
      END;
      IF B>C THEN B:=C;
      IF A>B THEN B:=A;
      MEDIAN:=B
      {MEDIAN CONTAINS THE DESIRED RESULT}
END.
```

4. ```
{A PL/T PROGRAM TO REVERSE A NUMBER}

VAR NUMBER,REBMUN,DIGIT;

BEGIN {SIMULATE INPUT OF NUMBER BY ASSIGNMENT}
      NUMBER:=142;
      {LOOP TO COMPUTE REVERSE OF NUMBER}
      REBMUN:=0;
      WHILE NUMBER<>0 DO
      BEGIN DIGIT:=NUMBER-(NUMBER/10)*10;
            NUMBER:=NUMBER/10;
            REBMUN:=REBMUN*10+DIGIT
      END
      {REBMUN CONTAINS THE DESIRED RESULT}
END.
```

8. ```
{A PL/T PROGRAM TO COMPUTE N-CHOOSE-R}

VAR N,R,NCR,I;

BEGIN {SIMULATE INPUT OF N,R BY ASSIGNMENT}
      N:=12; R:=2;
      {DETERMINE BEST VALUE FOR R, I.E. MIN(R,N-R)}
      IF R>(N-R) THEN R:=N-R;
      {COMPUTE N-CHOOSE-R}
      NCR:=1; I:=1;
      WHILE I<=R DO
      BEGIN NCR:=NCR*(N-I+1)/I; I:=I+1
      END
      {NCR CONTAINS DESIRED RESULT}
END.
```

70
```

References

1. Elsworth, E.F. (1979) Compilation via an Intermediate Language. *Computer Journal*, **22**, 226–233.
2. Amman, U. *et al. The Pascal P-Compiler: Implementation Notes*. ETH, Zurich.
3. *The UCSD p-System and UCSD Pascal Users' Manual* (1981) SofTech Microsystems Inc., San Diego, California.
4. Berry, R.E. (1978) Experience with the Pascal P-Compiler. *Software—Practice and Experience*, **8**, 617–627.
5. Wirth, N. (1976) *Algorithms + Data Structures = Programs* 1st edn. Prentice Hall, New Jersey.

Index

System Program Sections, Procedures and Functions

General Index

Page references in *italics* refer to figures, or to associated text and figures occuring on the same page.

Index

75

stack pointer (SP) register 11, 18, *19*, 20, 21
statement, source language
    EBNF grammar 15
    syntax diagram *17*
    translation of 22-24
STATEMENT procedure 10
STO instruction 20, 23
store addressing registers 11, *19*; *see also* PP; SB register; SP register
SUB instruction 20
SYM next source symbol 7, 8
syntax, source language 15-*17*
syntax analysis 5, 7-9
syntax checker
    definition 1
    see also PARSER program; PARSER0 program

table look-up 6, 9
target machine language 1
term, source language
    EBNF grammar 15
    syntax diagram *17*
    translation of 22-23
TERM procedure 9

top-of-stack pointer (SP) register 11, 18, *19*, 20, 21
TURBO Pascal 2, 25, 27

VALUE identifier target value *8*
variable (VAR) declaration, source language
    definition 3
    EBNF grammar 15
    syntax diagram *16*
    translation of 22
variable addressing registers 18, *19*; *see also* SB register; SP register
variables, calculation workspace 19
variables' 'undefined' initialization 11, 12
vocabulary, source language 13-14

WHILE statement, source language
    EBNF grammar 15
    syntax diagram *17*
    translation of *23*-24
Wirth, Niklaus 2
workspace stack mechanism 18, *19*, 20, 22-23